the nobody bible

the nobody bible

uncovering the simple wisdom in
ordinary life

J. A. Plosker

nobody
press

First Edition, 2017
Published by Nobody Press
USA

Nobody Press
NobodyPress.com
info@NobodyPress.com

Cover, book design, and illustrations by Nobody Press and MG Innovations, LLC.

This book is for entertainment and general informational purposes only. The author is not dispensing medical, mental health, or legal advice. Seek the advice of a qualified physician for any mental or physical health issue. If you use the information in this book for yourself, author and publisher assume no responsibility for your actions. While author and publisher made every attempt to verify this book's information, neither publisher nor author assume any liability for errors, omissions, post-publication changes, or contrary interpretations. Any perceived slight of an individual or organization is purely unintentional.

Print ISBN: 978-0-9987283-0-8
Ebook ISBN: 978-0-9987283-1-5

To M and M
Your love makes this nobody in particular feel like somebody special.

To all the faces in the crowd
Although your days may pass unnoticed, your good deeds and good thoughts are shared by us all.

Contents

The Book Before the Books

What's the Problem? Why Should We Care?

I'm just an ordinary person with a job and bills to pay who wanted to live a better life. Really original, right? When I made the decision, I wasn't living in the worst set of human circumstances by any stretch of the imagination. Still, I had anxieties, fears, and doubts. The usual stuff. The troublesome stuff. The stuff that plagues us when we're dwelling comfortably in the middle of the bell curve (see Fig. 1).

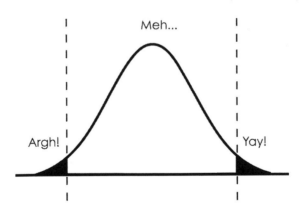

Fig. 1. Bell curve depicting my highly scientific view of the human condition.

My issues weren't headline news, but they were real enough to me. You know the old saying (that I made up just now): we tend to feel 100 percent of the weight of our own problems. I had so much I wanted to do, but so much junk inside holding me back. I had goals, but little direction. I was doing okay, but I knew there was so much more. I knew there were other faces in the crowd like me trying to get by, but it was really hard to connect across the miles of anonymity. And no, social media wasn't a super-efficient mechanism for networking. I mean, how would we seekers even find each other? How many people put, "Looking to make friends who are also feelin' the weight of *Weltschmerz*[1]" as a hobby in their profile?

Anyway, I kept on my path as best as I could—teaching my comparative religion and philosophy classes, writing, and doing my social work counseling. As I stumbled along, I started to become keenly aware of certain questions arising in me, and in folks around me, over and over again:

- Is there a doorway to a better life available right now?
- Do I have anything meaningful to contribute?
- I know I have a spark inside, but can anyone see it?
- Are there inner tools to ease my anxiety?
- What's personal growth, and should I be doing it?
- How can I be spiritual? What does that even mean?
- Should religion and spirituality be in my life?
- Isn't philosophical study just for crusty academics?
- Why create or improve if nobody knows who I am?

Infinite varieties of these questions poured out of students, clients, and *me*. Now that I'm more in tune to them, I hear their echoes on TV, in the news, and on the street. Amid these swirling uncertainties, we're all—apart and together—out there in the world trying to live our lives as best as we can: raising our families, working our jobs, trying to make meaningful connections, and just being who we are, even if we don't get recognition or credit. Even if nobody notices. And sometimes, if we lose ourselves for a moment along the way, we realize we're not exactly sure what we're doing or who, exactly, we're supposed to be. Perhaps we have a nagging need to improve our lives or take up a meaningful practice—spiritual or otherwise—but we don't know how. We don't know where to start. Or it could be that we just want to make a small life change or be better people (whatever that means). We might have anxiety we can't quite place or feel a subtle malaise that takes over our lives. Maybe we're just stuck. Our problems along the way don't make the headlines, but that doesn't make them any less real. Trust me.

Where can we turn for guidance, stability, and real help when there seems to be no anchors to keep us from drifting? Politicians switch with the seasons, TV shows and styles change on a whim, stars on social media dictate our morality, and it's all so confusing! Compasses keep shifting. No wonder so many of us have angst. Where are the (lasting) answers? How the heck do we find the right road? Do we need experts to point us in the right direction? There has to be a better way.

Look, we're living in difficult times. Stressful times. If someone tells you differently, check them for a pulse. Everything moves at lightning speed, and it's easy to feel left behind. We have a lot on our plates, yet we're always hungry. In so many ways, we're living in a time of division. Labels and word limits substitute for substance. It's a time of misunderstanding. A time when all our hair triggers seem to want to go off at once. It's certainly a time when it's so much easier to retreat into the safe and familiar (no matter what it looks like) than to engage and participate in the new. It's tempting to live with our pain and limitations because busting out beyond our borders is so scary. And really, all the fine advice from all the most enlightened gurus can ring hollow while the phone at work is ringing off the hook.

Is it all doom and gloom? Of course not! What am I, a monster? My point here is that sometimes, in the center of the tempest, it's really (really!) hard to see the rainbow on the horizon.

Here's how I've seen all this in action from one narrow strip of my life: I had religious studies and philosophy students who came to class searching for answers. Actually, most of them were searching for easy humanities credits, but some wanted real answers to their problems and mysteries. Many wanted to understand their personal situations so they could reach out and help others who were suffering. Many of my social work clients wanted a way out of addiction and mental health struggles. A lot of these folks were stuck in their lives because they had burning questions or suffered devastating life events, but had no idea how to make sense of it all. No idea how to move forward or move on. So many of these folks wanted answers from me—asking me point blank for solutions. But who was I to handle all of this? Just some guy with a few degrees showing up for a few hours. I was nobody in particular. After all, it was the clients and students who were living their lives. They were dealing with their issues. I could join their struggle for a time and listen with compassion and a desire to help. However, at the end of a session or day, I disconnected and made my way home through the crowd to my own personal issues.

But I was the expert, right? I was supposed to be the person with the answers, right? I had the background in religion, philosophy, and counseling, right? I could hardly help myself! What now? I knew these good people with great questions had to find their own answers if they wanted any lasting, meaningful progress. Although I couldn't provide specific advice on any one person's approach to peace, health, or healing, I realized that I did have something to offer: my unique point of view from my own search. We all have collected wisdom from our lives, and we can share it, even when it seems like we have nothing to give. So here it is: *no matter who you are, if there's something you want to create or improve in your life—whether it's better grades, inner peace, good mental health, or whatever—keep the tools simple and authentic.*

The first key is *simplicity*. Try to find those tools in the life you're living. In the ordinary. The solutions to the myriad of life-altering puzzles aren't generally found by getting more complex, but by stripping away layers of complexity and taking stock of what's around you. For example, if you want to explore religion or spirituality as a transformational tool, then instead of getting lost in a labyrinth of harsh dogma, religious politicking, guru-jumping, and all the other things we feel we must do to "get it right" or "get the truth," find what is simple and familiar in religion, philosophy, spirituality, and good ol' fashioned humanity, and start the search there. If you jump right in to conversion, dietary restrictions, memorizing holy books, etc., chances are you won't transform—you'll burn out! Start small. Start humbly. Start in the everyday. Target the desired change and use the simplest tool. Learn a little. Explore a little. Attend a service. Talk to some folks. Meditate for a few minutes and follow breath as it enters your body. Watch your thoughts. Take a small step into the dimly lit areas around you instead of a giant leap into the dark. If your problems require something more, then by all means, do something more. But just remember at the outset: a shovel will dig the hole for your plant just fine. You don't need dynamite.

In addition to sweet simplicity, a seeker on any path must embrace his or her *authentic* identity. Isn't it easier to just be who you are each day instead of trying to be someone or something you're not? It's tempting to make the term "authentic" complicated and murky—as if it's something that is lost and must be found. But it boils down to this: be who you really are. For example, if you love poetry and being loud, it's better to go to poetry slams at bars than to sit quietly in a library reading verses. Be you. Just you. Remember that whole thing about being simple? Apply it here. The easiest course is the genuine course. If you decide to change, that's fine, but start from who you are instead of who others think you should be. First be real, then get to work on your search. That's the way to find diamonds of wisdom in the world's coal.

Now, pay attention to this next one, because it's very important. When folks on a search say things to me like, "What do I know about this stuff?" or "I don't understand religion or philosophy enough to make sense of my life," I say: *you don't have to be an expert to make positive change or improvement.* To create a better life, you don't have to be a scholar, saint, newspaper-recognized hero, living legend, or perfect parent. There's no need to be innocent of all crimes, wealthy, or famous. The wisdom available to the great dwellers of Olympus is also available to the rest of us. Right here. Right now. Right in this classroom. Right in this therapy session. Right in this life. Tests, quizzes, drugs, rap sheets, diplomas, and perceptions aside, we all have access to the greatest gifts. Now. The most useful wisdom is not complex and elusive, dressed in elaborate robes and known only to the lucky few. No. It is hiding in plain sight in unassuming clothes and walking shoes. Maybe we believe that the loftiest solutions—spiritual, religious, or otherwise—are reserved for those at the loftiest heights. But that's simply not true. The dwellers on high may occasionally toss down useful pearls, but y'know? There's plenty of oysters for the picking down here at sea level.

Got all that? Really? You're good. It took me years to figure it out. Let's just review one more time. If you want to improve your life, make a positive change, or create something new:

- Keep the tools simple
- Be authentic on your search
- Remember: no wealth, fame, or ordination is necessary

Easy, right? Not exactly. It takes practice and patience. Simplicity takes discipline, and that's not always easy to come by. Just like my students, clients, and everyone else on this planet, I am on my own journey of the soul, spirit, energy thing, or whatever it is. I'm seeking to improve and live a more authentic life. I have my own issues and my own doubts about my abilities to affect meaningful change or to create something in my life. I fall short a lot of the time. But I focus on that formula you just read, and I practice it as best as I can. How did I discover it? Well, that's the story of *The Nobody Bible*.

When I got really serious about change, I sought guidance in my library of collected wisdom and reflected on my studies in religion, spirituality, and the mind. I realized that so much of what I had learned through outside investigation was really in me all along—simple, plain, and available. I came to understand that the course of an ordinary life is more than just a series of days on a rambling calendar. It is actually a tool to help me figure out who I really am and deal with my "nows" and "thens" in a much more calm, focused, and genuine way. And by the way, this device is tailored specifically for me—just as yours is for you. You see, there isn't one answer for all of us. Instead, the world provides myriad answers for each one of us, individually. It presents us with unique connections, custom points of view, and the opportunity to improve each and every day. Even though I don't have fame or vast wealth, I do have my everyday experiences. And you know what?

The famous figures of the traditions we're going to discuss in this book didn't all start out renowned or remarkable. Nope. Many were regular (okay, sometimes royal) folks who began with nothing but their daily lives. They were carpenters, caravan drivers, and herders. They had no platform at the beginning. No crowds cheering at the starting line. No viral videos. They were just people, with a life to live and a journey to take. They were folks who found something amazing right in the life and times in which they lived. That was all the inspiration I needed.

Think of it this way: God[2] didn't send Moses to free the Hebrews from Pharaoh's heavy hand because Moses was an expert in Egyptian hieroglyphics. The Buddha wasn't destined to show the way to enlightenment because he had a doctorate in metaphysics. Jesus didn't teach through parables because he was professor of communication and parable studies at the Hebrew University. Great religious and philosophical figures are indeed great in retrospect, but perhaps they were great because they came from the crowd (in some cases it was a royal crowd, but still…). They were people on the outs, people of unknown origin, or people hidden away. They were sometimes lost, sometimes searching, sometimes full of doubt. They connected with a god, other people, or whatnot through authenticity and sincerity. They connected through emotion. They connected through grace. Whatever tools they had or whatever it was they were good at—moving sheep around, selling goods, ruling, or building things—it was certainly enough to get them started on their world missions. No matter your background or where you are now, you can do this, too. You do do this. (Doo doo be doo!)

If you're still with me and you still care, then just know that this book is nothing more than one ordinary person's attempt to identify a path for better living. It's a collection of insights discovered (so far) as I try to be myself and figure it all out. *The Nobody*

Bible will reveal how you can access simple, ancient, and powerful tools for personal change and growth right in the life you have. How? Well, consider this: the world's religious traditions, at their cores, were meant to provide roadmaps to peace and transformation. You can follow these roadmaps right in your everyday life, no matter who you are or what you believe. There are already techniques and suggestions out there that can profoundly impact our lives, and we do them every single day—whether we know it or not.

I know that all sounds very grand and ambitious, so let me just say at the outset that this book can't offer you wealth or instant enlightenment. However, it can hand you a few coins for the purse or some candles for the darkness.

On this journey, you'll:

- Explore religion, spirit, and philosophy
- Discover the extraordinary wisdom in ordinary life
- (Hopefully) laugh once or twice
- Gain the confidence to ask and answer tough questions
- Exercise your brain and do a little homework (gasp!)
- Discover that you have more in common with your neighbors around this globe than you think

As we go along, you will be asked to be authentic, brave, simple, and honest. You'll learn a little about me (if you care—or, you can skip my stories), but I'm hoping you'll learn a lot more about you. In that spirit, I'm going to use "I," "we," "you," and "us" as we move along, because I want this book to be a communal exercise where we're all in it together.

On the way, I'm going to show you that you, as you are right now, are wise and on a very potent path to, well, whatever you want. Maybe I'll even convince you that through simple, ordinary actions, you are already living out history's most influential and impactful wisdom and cooking up ancient recipes for personal growth. I have some fun exercises planned and a complete chapter (*The Book of You*) that you'll fill in on your own. It's dedicated entirely to your own point of view. On that note, I want to issue an invitation for you to visit us at thenobodybible.com where you can find downloadable versions of all the exercises in this book, including *The Book of You*. That way, you ebook readers (or paperback readers who would like more room) can print it all out and fill it in when you want.

Oh, and before we get started, please remember a few things: my background in religious studies (and a touch of philosophy) doesn't make me an expert on all the wonderful ways these traditions can guide you. My years as a counselor don't give me license to judge what goes on in your head.[3] My personal religious or spiritual beliefs have no bearing on your belief or lack thereof. In fact, I don't consider myself an expert in anything except my own life. I know what length I like my hair, and I know I love eighties music. I know I don't like stewed tomatoes, and you telling me how delicious your great-grandmother's recipe is won't change that a bit. I know that sunshine (on my shoulder or elsewhere) makes me feel pretty great, and the fact that John Denver knew it first is just a coincidence. In other words, I know what I like and what makes me tick. You'll have to keep your own counsel about what better living and authenticity means to you.

We are who we are, and we are wise as we are, even if nobody knows who we are. And that makes us just as ripe and ready for a better life as anyone else in this world.

The Book of Beginnings

Religion, Spirit, and What to Expect

Teaching comparative religion is tough. It requires a person to do things of which mama disapproved. Remember? She told you that it's not polite to discuss religion or politics in a group. Well, in my classes we often go well beyond the polite, venturing into the downright dirty. We don't just look at religion behind glass like the Mona Lisa. We don't tuck in our napkins and remain seen but not heard. We don't sit with hands folded, feet on the floor, talking in our best inside voice. We engross ourselves in religion, even if only for an hour. We defend it, dissect it, question it, prop it up, and knock it down. We stuff the shirt with hay, jam the scarecrow in the ground, and let the crows peck at its eyes. Then we burn the whole thing down and do it all over again. And again. Tradition after tradition. This isn't a museum, for goodness sake. It's study. It's life. It matters to us!

I say "us" because I feel very strongly that religious discourse and study should be a community project where people come together to explore and better understand a phenomenon so pervasive, it touches everyone in society. We have no choice but to study it because no matter one's opinion of the religious, religion itself is more than an occasional occurrence. Oh, and don't even get me started on spirituality. I'll dive into that deep end and bang my head later.

Religious ritual, doctrine, and belief are phenomena one will encounter every step of the way in this life, so it's important to investigate where we can. And since this book will rely heavily on the tenets of world religion—and because so much of how we understand others and ourselves depends on it—I think it's important to start out with a brief discussion. Do you agree? Good! Let's go.

You're in It! Even If You Don't Want It!

Although this book doesn't require belief in any particular religion, everyone has a relationship to religion whether they subscribe to one or not. If you are in a religion (but not particularly religious), perhaps you participate in the rituals and holidays out of habit or respect or have a family to whom the religious path is particularly important. Maybe that ol' Catholic or Jewish guilt—the hidden pillar of many other religions by the way—rears its head from time to time, reminds you of your heritage, and draws you back. If you are not in one—say, an atheist—then your lack of a belief in a god or gods might lead you to take a position against the trappings of religion or state that you'd prefer to be free of or apart from it in your daily life. That's a relationship. When you take a position in relation to something (for, against, or apart), you acknowledge it and give it wings to soar or claws to defend. Debating the merits or limitations of religion animates it. Your presence or absence gives it existence. By the way, indifference is also a position in case you thought you could escape that easily. A willow is likely indifferent to the existence of wind, but it bends in the breeze nonetheless.

There is religion and religious symbolism all around you. It may not always take a form you recognize, but it's there. You can take it for granted or not notice it at all, but it is present nevertheless. That tree we just mentioned still rustles its leaves even if you aren't there to hear it. Religion is on your money, in your novels, and on bumper stickers and billboards across the land. It changes minds, sways opinions, and keeps people in line even when they are living in solitude. When you watch election returns, become engrossed in a *Star Wars* movie marathon eagerly awaiting Yoda's teachings, turn away from a closed drycleaner on Sunday with your soiled suit in your hand, stand for the Pledge of Allegiance, pray for a job interview to go well, observe a federal holiday, watch a ballplayer point to the heavens after a grand slam, or have a friend who tells you he can't eat a cheeseburger or drink a beer, you are, quite possibly, interfacing with religion. You are encountering the *religious*. Remember that.

Yes, Even Tradition Changes

Religion isn't a static, unchanging monolith. Religion is an eclectic, colorful quilt where folks can, if they're so inclined, mix and match patterns and styles. Some people participate in more than one path. I've had folks tell me that they feel on the outs with family or friends for taking a Buddhist worldview to church or for investigating *Kabbalah* (Jewish mysticism) even though they are not Jewish. But who says we have to eat one flavor of ice cream? And if someone (such as an ardent devotee) says it, who says we should listen?

The story of religion is a story of change, exploration, and growth. It's okay to mix and explore. But then again, stories of mixing and transformation often meet resistance. In fact, mixing can lead to upheaval! No trailblazer in a high-stakes history of change had it easy (Jesus, anyone?). The same goes for us. If you want color, variety, good ol' exploration, or to just go your own way entirely, sometimes you will be considered the jester and not the king. That doesn't mean you are what others think, but you will be to others what they perceive. Are you still willing to put yourself out there in the green bodysuit and jingling hat? Do you have the courage to walk your own path even when you're walkin' all by your lonesome?

Mixing, blending, and questioning are nothing new, just in case you do this and are feeling alone. A study from the Pew Research Center[1] indicates that religious beliefs and practices are increasingly defying categorization. Interesting, right? In other words, people are mixing it up out there. They're merging Eastern and Western paths and talking more about the New Age, ghosts, astrology, and energy. Yeah, that latter stuff may not be wholly religious, but it shows that people are opening their minds to things. A study of 35,000 adults showed the percentage who believe in a god, pray, or regularly attend religious services is declining.[2] That's not good or bad. It just is. People are out there in the world doing religion their way. Or not at all. That's fine! Oh, and one more nugget. Another study reveals that one in five adults in the U.S. were raised in interfaith homes.[3] Yep. Twenty percent of us are from religiously blended families.

Still feel out of place if you mix traditions, explore, or have eclectic beliefs? Still don't think religious discussions are important and evolving? You're still not convinced this matters? How about these stats from Pew: one third of Americans say they regularly attend religious services at more than one place. Oh, and another third do it on occasion. And the kicker? About a quarter say they go to services at a faith different from their own.[4]

It doesn't matter if you are a Protestant sitting with your wife at Catholic Mass or a Buddhist going to synagogue with your Jewish girlfriend. Times are changing, folks. Lines are blurring. People are reading. Fingers are surfing the internet. The world is getting smaller. The neatly outlined, color-coded map you used to see in class with all the different countries labeled by religion (if you, like me, are of a certain age) is quickly morphing into a wildly abstract spectacle that Jackson Pollock would envy. Get that. Know that. Understand that. You are in that fantastic marbled madness now! That reality is outside your door, even if it is not inside your home or your heart. Get to know others and what they believe. They're getting to know you.

I don't know your religious affiliation, your views on god(s), or your holiday calendar. However, I'm telling you all of this at the outset because I believe the study of religion is important outside the borders of the university, as it forms a framework of society whether you are a believer or not. It matters.

Give That Definition Some Muscle, Or Else Put Some Muscle in That Definition!

All of this chatter and ado about the word "religion." Religion, religion, religion. But what exactly is it? You'd think a term so important would have an ancient definition chiseled in a cave in Galilee or China that would clear the whole thing up and make it all rock solid and set in the hardest of stone.

Not so much.

There are many definitions of religion—some proffered by laymen, some proffered by PhDs—but all problematic to one person or another. Don't miss that last point. See it clearly. Religion, as something so often defined and so very foundational to so many people's existence, is something difficult to define. What a way to start out, right? Don't blame me. I didn't spill it. I'm just mopping it up with one of those soggy mops you wring out by hand. Gross. Who uses those anymore? Anyway, we can't start this journey into

The Nobody Bible without a definition of religion, right? After all, it's a book that's going to illustrate how teachings from some of the world's major religions can help us on our way through life. So let's try to get something going here that can guide us a little. Or confuse us. Whatever.

At the outset, understand that religious definition is prone to bias. In other words, how a practitioner in California defines it might be different than how a practitioner in India defines it. They may both meditate in an *ashram* (a place for religious retreat and learning), but when it comes to defining what they're doing, they may not agree. If we include in the definition one almighty and all-powerful God (with a capital "G"), we risk excluding too much— say, religions that have many gods or no god (with a little "g").

"Huh?" you ask. You heard me.

Understand this: we often take definitions for granted in our own lives without considering that what may be obvious to us is not always obvious to someone else. We often consider our point of view to be gospel truth until we are asked to consider another viewpoint. Then the view gets hazy. You have your Jesus, Shiva, or Tao, but someone else has her Siddhartha. He says a blessing over bread and wine at Friday services, and she takes communion a few times a year. That couple over there just exchanged wedding vows on the beach with an officiant who was ordained online and is wearing flip-flops. She wants to merge with her personal and loving God, while he meditates without concern for any god. He left the religious building behind because he doesn't think ritual and formality are necessary, and she can't pray without bending the knee in front of a Catholic altar. My goodness! Which parts of this mish-mash are considered religious? Are some of the people in these examples more religious than others?

Forget It! Define It However You Want!

In light of that flurry of activity I just described, I've decided something. I'm not going to provide you with a definitive defini- tion of religion. Surprise! I make it a point to avoid conflict, so this seems like a good occasion to practice that. I hope you're not too disappointed. Here's my reasoning, and I think it's sound: rather than shoehorn us all into one neat and tidy cardboard box with the flaps that never seem to fold in correctly, I am going to leave you to your own good graces and intelligence to figure it out for yourself as we go, albeit with some guidelines.

Before we get to those guidelines, however, I want you to ponder a few things. When you set about the practice of defining religion for yourself, remember that you are unintentionally defining it for others—at least as you'll view them and their practices through your lens. Through definition, you will include yourself and exclude others whether you mean to or not. Try to suspend the we-versus-they mentality as best you can while you read this book, and try to be open to differences. Try to be forgiving. Try to understand that even if what you are about to read in the following pages fails to conform to your more formal definitions (or those of your rabbi, imam, minister, or guru), it doesn't mean that it won't conform for the person on the train next to you.

Consider this: let's pretend you and I go on a safari. Our guide tells us the general route and some of the animals to watch out for. However, we have no idea what we'll see. I'm excited to encounter the elephants, but you are positively bonkers for birds. My videos of the trip are full of furry, four-legged folks. You? Feathered friends. We both have a great time, and we both feel we had the experience we wanted. In the end, "safari" wasn't a defined set of encounters that came pre-packaged. Instead, the term came to mean something different to both of us. In fact, each tourist in our tiny caravan will construct his or her own meaning of the safari based on preferences and a personal experience of the journey— through animals, people, trees, foods, smells, sights, and sounds. It was the meditative chirping of crickets at night or the quiet grazing of zebras during the day. Or perhaps it was new cultures, new recipes, or colorful crafts from an amazing country. It was something different for everybody. Maybe someone describes the trip as a "religious experience." What does that mean? Who knows? It's a feeling. Something deep and indescribable that likely defies definition. Think about that. Or not.

Let's Get on with the Guidelines!

Okay, now the guidelines I promised. With the previous example in mind, consider these offerings from the great definitional safari. Take personal snapshots of what you want, and as for everything else? Just buy a postcard. When you consider what religion is, think of a lens through which believers view their worlds and find meaning in their life journeys. Think of people performing rituals, such as lighting candles or honoring ancestors. Think about people following rules, such as avoiding certain foods on certain days. Consider gods (or lack thereof) and founders (or, again, lack thereof). When you think you have a definition in mind, remember that it is your mind. Your definition. Then, think again. Maybe it doesn't matter how we define religion. Maybe it's about how we live out what we believe, and whether we consider it religious or not.

Based on what we now know, maybe your personal attempt at a definition of religion goes something like this: *I believe religion is something that helps people to get through their daily troubles. Religions probably have some kind of god or spirit thing that watches over their particular group, and the group believes they have some kind of special or divine purpose. There's probably some important book in there that someone received from a divine source. Maybe two or three books. Oh, and you have to do certain stuff on certain days so that you are in line with some kind of sacred calendar or something—like when boys become men or girls become women or we eat some kind of meat dish or gelatin thing with fruit pieces in it. There is also all-you-can-eat pasta and breadsticks, but the salad is extra.*

That's a start! Your definition will include some traditions, exclude (and confuse) others, and make your Italian family happy. Not everyone will agree with it, but it gives you a jumping-off point. A reference. Something to talk about at a party. As for something more concrete? Sorry. This is probably the best I can do. Good luck, and good eating![5]

Religious? I'm More Spiritual. And I'm Still Not Comfortable with the Whole "God" Thing.

How many times have you heard someone say, "I'm not religious. I'm more spiritual"? That phrase is so common now, it's...well...common. But there really is a distinction there, and it's important. For years, I've been studying, developing, and failing at spiritual practices. For me, a real biggie is saying mantras and repeating special learning points to myself through the day. For others, it might be seated meditation, walking in the woods, or cutting off their split ends.

Early on in my personal journey, I made friends again with a key distinction. Spirituality (to me) is subjective. It isn't something "out there." Instead, it's a personal feeling of connection with something bigger, and it takes place inside me. As for religion? Well, it became the paradoxical objective—out there in the world somewhere. It's the house of worship I enter, the pre-printed prayers in the dusty book, and the list of things from thousands of years ago that I should embrace or avoid. I say religion is *paradoxically* objective because it is certainly out there in the world in the form of rule, ritual, and structure, but it can also foster a connection with the deep and personal self within. That last part is no small point. Spirituality can be a highly individual and personal experience, but religion can help foster that internal connection. For example, if a person takes communion in remembrance of Christ, perhaps a feeling of overwhelming peace descends upon him—a peace that he takes to the yoga studio later in the day. If someone fasts on a certain religious holiday, perhaps their hunger gets them in better touch with what really matters in life—spurring them to volunteer at a food bank or keep a gratitude journal. As I've learned, even studying the foundations of religion (without actually practicing or believing in them all) can build a spiritual connection. I guess it's like watching an inspiring film. The movie is out there on the screen, and we're not actually part of the unfolding saga. However, it ignites emotions deep within us that can affect our lives long after the lights come on and we leave the theater.

Do you have to be religious or spiritual (whatever those mean) to benefit from the teachings of religion and spirituality (whatever those are)? I don't think so. This book doesn't think so, either. But that's just me. You're you. You do you. Whatever you choose to believe, just know that you can be spiritual or religious (or neither!), and they can be intertwined (or not!). That's important, because it means that your tour of world traditions has no jacket required. We'll talk more about these concepts throughout the book, so don't forget this little conversation.

Hey, Relax! You've Got This.

Enough of the super-heavy stuff. Let's move on and prepare for the journey we're about to take together. *The Nobody Bible* isn't going to prove that a particular god does or does not exist. I'm not interested in convincing anyone of anything supernatural. After all, who am I to say what is right and what is wrong on the god-score? I'm just a nobody with some opinions. It's in the heart where personal proof of the great and ultimate resides—in your heart with your threshold of belief. It's deep in the self where convincing takes place. Your self. To argue the rightness and wrongness of such a personal subject seems ludicrous. I'll leave that for the somebodies on those religious radio and TV shows. Your conception of god, spirit, or your life purpose is whatever you want it to be. This is your adventure.

Speaking of choosing an adventure, did you ever read those books when you were a kid? You remember. The ones that let you take a path through the book to create your own story. If you haven't, you should. I can't be sure, but I think my parents may have sold my cherished collection at a garage sale in the eighties along with my Atari gaming system, a beloved stuffed animal, and a few other things I now wish I had back. Too bad. Those books were good fun. In case you don't remember them, here's the skinny. Say the theme is the Old West. You might be the small-town sheriff who enters the smoky, crowded saloon. Across the saw-dusted floor, the bad guy is at the bar. His back is to you, a silver gun cradled in a worn leather holster. He's wearing a smug look of indifference, casually swirling his whiskey. A gnarly cigar dangles from his cracked lips, raining ashes onto the distressed bar top. It's tense. Your long search is over, and the danger's begun. It's real. It's decision time. Do you call out the bad guy's name right then and there so you can try to be the hero? Or do you risk a few precious minutes to assemble the posse and call the villain out to the street where he'll be outmanned and outgunned? Choose a path from two choices and turn to that page. Read your fate. You were shot dead in the door of the saloon. Crap. But good news! Just flip back a few pages, start over, and choose a different path. Go get that posse. They're probably smoking and drinking at another bar.

It's no one else's business to read over your shoulder and decide your life for you. Take the joy the story has to offer, make your own decision, and, if you find it wanting, choose another way to go. I'd rather live in the mystery than argue it to death. Where the hell's the fun in that?

It's All About the Bible, Huh?

I use the term "Bible" in the book title, even though it contains a Western bias. But right here is a chance to broaden our horizons. See, Bible is a flexible word. Yes, it can be capitalized and refer to the central religious text so familiar to the Jewish and Christian traditions. However, in ordinary usage, it can also mean a cornerstone or foundational text. We may have a certain cookbook that has a spot-on recipe for chocolate cake the way our family likes. We may call that cookbook our dessert bible. Or how about that fantastic textbook that explains a math problem just right? (By the way, if you find that book, tell me. I never did.) That may be a bible as well. Some people have worn out copies of *The Catcher in the Rye*, *The Celestine Prophecy*, or some other work from a favorite author, and that might be their bible. Why? Because it was a support for them during a difficult time. Or perhaps it gave just the right advice in just the right amount at just the right moment—like a Pez dispenser when you have a craving for sugary chalk. Maybe your bible represents a time or a place or a feeling that is a cornerstone in your life.

Well, this is a nobody's bible (which, by the way, sounded much better than *The Nobody Pez Dispenser*). It's *my* bible, of sorts. It represents years of study and ongoing self-investigation. It is a reference for when anxieties get a little out of control. It represents one often-undisciplined man's disciplined search for knowledge and his attempts to apply it in the real world—sometimes successfully, and at other times...well...that's what second editions are for, right?

Now listen folks, I know the religions of the world are as complex and diverse as each unique follower. I know you probably have your own spiritual practices and religious attachments. You have a personal connection to your highest philosophies and principles and you may also have formal rituals that plug you in to those principles. I know there is a lot more out there that can be said for each of these traditions and for your personal journeys, and I know that I am not going to cover everything that may be important to you. A lot has been left out, for sure. But this isn't a religious studies textbook or sacred text, alright? It's probably not Jesus the way you know him and it may not be the Confucian values you were brought up with. It may not agree with your yoga teacher's lectures or your guru's thoughts on things (however, since he's a guru, he's already forgiven me as an example to you on forgiveness). But in many ways, that is the spirit of this book. Think of it like a used car: it isn't comfortable for everyone, it doesn't come with an ironclad warranty, and it may not always drive straight. But it can get you a few miles down the road. And if not? Well, you can trade it in for something else. There's plenty to choose from out there.

Enough with the Babble. What's in It for Me?

We've touched on this briefly, but let's really set the stage on the most vital question: why read this book instead of wrapping fish in it? Or for the ebook readers among you, why swipe through it with your index finger instead of playing a game on your device that lets you match candy or farm animals or whatever for virtual treasure?

Well first, let's talk about what this book isn't going to do and what it's not about. It's not going to teach you to speak with the departed or become an overnight sensation in a particular field. It isn't a grand debate on the merits of religion or one religion versus another. It doesn't decry science or push you to the nunnery. It's not a theological argument or a fiery attempt to prove the existence of anything other than your own life. It's not going to give you a comprehensive understanding of every religious tradition (good luck with that!). It's not going to remove wrinkles, strip away gray, or cover bald spots, and it won't magically and mystically transport you to a remote castle full of 11-year-old kids brandishing wands and casting potentially deadly spells. By the way, whose idea was that?

What you will find in these pages is lively discussion and some tools for personal development. Think of it like a big bag of fertilizer (a bunch of crap, right?) and some seeds. The book is the fertilizer and the religions are the seeds. Wait...is that right? I've used so many metaphors in this chapter that I'm getting all confused. Is it the other way around? No. No, I have it the right way: book equals fertilizer, religions equal seeds. Or maybe you are the seed. Anyway, there are some facts about the world's great religious traditions and some of their major figures. You'll read about what this particular nobody in particular thinks are some of the cornerstone teachings of these traditions, and you'll have a chance to provide your take on them. There are spiritual nuggets, philosophical diversions, mystical musings, meandering meditations, activities, and some reading selections. Oh, and a surprise appearance by a really cool Greek philosopher. And you'll hopefully discover that much of what you seek to make your life better is already in you and around you. The rest of the trip is simply what you see along the trail and what you truck in on your back. Please pack your garbage out with you.

Wait! Wait! A Few Additional Details.

Here are some last-minute housekeeping items: if you want, read this book alone and enjoy. If you fall asleep, just call it meditation time. If you so desire, you can get a bunch of folks together and read it in a group. Heck, you can all get together and pretend to read it. Hey, it's an excuse to get out of the house for a night and generally give the impression that you are getting yourself all cultured up with books. Next, I'd like you to really take your time with the exercises in each chapter as you go along. They aren't so short as to be a waste or so long as to be tedious. And there's no math! They are there to get you to engage the material and figure some things out. If you are diligent and honest with them, then at the end of the book you can compile the information you jotted down and create a Nobody Bible (or whatever you want to call it) of your very own. Neat, huh? And I want to repeat this: you can download the exercises over at thenobodybible.com.

Oh, and have fun. Why? Because a good time and a better life for a regular person (me!) out there in the world was the point of this experiment. I gathered resources together and found that the process was really a blast. It still is. I laughed at myself, I cried on myself, and I think I even drooled on my keyboard once or twice. I want you and your loved ones to have that same experience, but without the drool. See? You're having fun already! So much of religion, spirit, and study is serious and boring. Let's take a different approach, okay? I'll be sharing some funny stuff from my own life along the way so you won't feel alone.

And one last thing. I always made it a rule that clients and students don't have to participate if they don't want to. They can just take it in if that feels natural. And that's fine, really, as far as it goes. But you know? Participation is what builds confidence and uncovers insight. It also connects us. How? Well, I don't know you and you don't know me. But we are connected by this book-bridge, and that is something special. Now, go beyond that. Broaden the image as wide as you can. Imagine as you read that you are connecting with others in communities around the globe. Picture yourself spanning time and space, having a dialogue not just with the folks in your family, friend circle, book group, or fake get-out-of-the-house-for-an-hour book group, but that you are participating in something bigger. Something grander. Something in which even a nobody in particular can make a helluva difference. And by the end, you might find that you do more, know more, and are more than you ever imagined. Read in peace. Learn in love. Take in stride.

The Book of Beginnings Meditation

May I realize my true nature and be in harmony with it. May I have the patience to allow, the wisdom to discern, and the smarts to known when enough is enough. I am myself for good or for ill, and I am my own biggest fan, for better or worse. A loving understanding of this fact will bring more peace than a thousand fair-weather friends. Who needs 'em?

NOBODY'S BEGINNING EXERCISES

1. Did you have a preconceived notion of religion when you picked up this book? What do you think about the difficulty of defining religion? Does it surprise you?

2. Do you think religious beliefs are necessary to living a good life? How do you define a good life?

3. Are there experts you look to in a certain field? Why do you respect them? Do you consider yourself an expert in a particular area? Is purported expertise alone enough to garner respect or is there something more?

4. Fill in the prompt below with your own definition.

    My definition of religion:

    Below, please write your own meditation or something you can say each day if you need a pick-me-up (you'll be asked to do these in subsequent chapters, so practice up!):

The Book of Buddha

Is It Really All About the Suffering?

There is a story in the annals of history that is quite well known to so many, but also quite underappreciated by so many more. It is a story of searching and sacrifice, extinguishing and enlightenment. It is the story of a man who commissioned a glorious and prosperous mission of education and compassion to the world—a mission that did not involve guns, violence, or hatred. No, it's not about the author of this book. It's the story of a man named Siddhartha Gautama (563-486 B.C.E.).[1] You know him as Buddha.

There are many nuances to this story. Now, when I say "story," I am referring to a *sacred* story. A sacred history, so to speak. Essentially, a sacred story is a historical narrative meant to imbue believers with a sense of faith—faith that can bind a community (your religion professor probably has a different definition). Maybe there is a hint of the fantastic or the miraculous. Think of your own life. What are the stories you tell to family and friends or the tales you hear from them? Come on, think! You can come up with something.

I'll help you. What about that story your great grandparents told at their eighty-ninth wedding anniversary? You know. It's the one where they met on a farm in a faraway land. They had just turned twelve one day apart and were married just one short month later—all the while insisting they never laid eyes on one other person of the opposite sex, including their parents, until that moment. Do you have a cousin whose university antics have reached mythical status? He's the guy who could down a six-pack and a large pizza in sixty seconds and smoke two packs of cigarettes all before his morning chemistry class. Was that fish you wrestled with for an hour off the coast of Mexico really as big as you say? Did you really do battle with that kid in third grade or did you just trade slaps for a few seconds before running away and crying under the slide? When your mom describes that hill she climbed to get to school every day, are you sure it wasn't just a speed bump? Sure, people get married, do crazy things in college, catch fish, become embroiled in schoolyard tussles, and climb hills. The question is, is it always just as we remember or just as we heard it? Or is there something added for effect? Have you ever embellished a set of facts to win an argument or prove your case? Have you ever purposefully left bland facts out to make the remaining story ingredients tastier? Or added ingredients to cover for a less desirable taste?

As is the case with so many sacred stories, facts and accounts change over time as the dust of age and agenda settles in around the pillars of history. Life happens. People change things. Devotees add things. We can't always know for sure if something in these grand stories did or did not happen. But if that's true, what's the point of such a narrative? Can we believe anything we hear from the religious storyteller?

Maybe. Maybe not. The best we can do is fit together an account of a life from the puzzle pieces that come down to us through time. Then it is a matter of comparison, argument, archaeology, and—dare I say—guessing. Maybe we have to place the corner pieces first or fill in the picture in the middle where a piece seems to be missing. It's not all scientific. Don't believe me? Well, then think about the last time you told a funny story at guys' night out about a recent blind date. Was it really that bad? Maybe you were the problem that night, and a few extra false tidbits hide that fact. Or maybe your bachelorette party in Vegas wasn't exactly like the movies, but that's an inside joke between you and your pals. No one needs to know it was a thousand pennies you won from that slot machine. Let it be a thousand quarters. A thousand's a thousand, right? How many times in your narrations do people jump in to correct you, add a fact, or color the story?

Can We Stay on Topic, Please? What About the Buddha?

So yes. Getting back to the Buddha. What can we say about him? Well, to understand the Buddha's teachings, one must understand from whence they come. I remember encountering Buddha's story in my college days when I was a more apathetic sort of person. It didn't mean much to me then. It wasn't until my own determined research years later that I came to appreciate the religious wrangling of India in the sixth and fifth centuries before the Common Era. It made me think of the United States in the 1960s— another period in history to which I was no witness, but which holds a certain status of ferment and experimentation and a definite fascination for me. I always thought that if I could build a time machine, I would go back to the 1960s. And probably not for the reasons you think. (Alright...maybe for some of the reasons you think.)

Does it surprise you to know that Siddhartha, who would become Buddha, was not born into a life of poverty? I ask this because if you know something of his later life and his legacy, it is something of a story of renunciation and material sparseness. Ever met a Buddhist monk? They don't exactly drive sports cars. In his youth, he wanted for nothing. He didn't need to beg for a meal or pray for a roof over his head. He didn't have an early-life desire to find enlightenment, as it wasn't anything to which he was introduced. And that was by design.

As we said, legend and fact often bleed together in historical watercolor when it comes to sacred stories. Therefore, we must pick a version of Buddha's life and go with it. In light of that, let me reiterate a rule—if you disagree with accounts in this book, do not seek me out to yell at me. If you want to talk about it calmly, we can, but if you are the angry type, please find another way to channel it. Anyway, according to one tale or another, Siddhartha was born a prince of the Shakya clan, a tribe from what is modern-day Nepal. Some say his birth was particularly auspicious, owing to certain signs, including his mother Maya's dream that a white elephant entered her side to mark the moment of his conception. Some legends also say that he was born from his mother's side, which I guess is more comfortable than the Greek goddess Athena's birth from Zeus's head. Siddhartha's mother died a week after his birth.

A wise man inspected the infant Siddhartha and told Siddhartha's father that the boy was destined to be great in one of two ways: either he would inherit his father's kingdom and be a great leader, or, if Siddhartha witnessed suffering, he would become a great spiritual teacher. Guess which one his father wanted? You got it. The king took great pains to keep Siddhartha from seeing or experiencing suffering. It is said the young Siddhartha was kept behind walls in a prison of luxury. He had palaces, temptations, and delights galore—something to which many of today's up-and-coming politicians aspire. He was married off at an early age to tie him to the domestic life, and he had a son. According to duties of his caste, or Hindu[2] station in life, Siddhartha was trained in warring arts and groomed to take his father's place on the throne.

As it is with the best-laid plans of history, something happened along the way that planted seeds of doubt in an unknowingly fertile mind. One of the great religious leaders of history was thrust into the spotlight—not because of a shove from encouraging onlookers, but rather, because he deliberately took his leave from the stage. It is said that Siddhartha longed to leave the palace grounds and to see the world that had for so long been locked away from him. His father reluctantly relented, but instructed the carriage driver to avoid the pains of the world so that the young Siddhartha would remain in ignorance. We are told that the town was decorated in all beauty so that a seamless path of peace could be drawn from the palace grounds into the waiting world. But reality finds a way, seeping through the cracks and catching us unaware in our delusions. On his brief journey, Siddhartha saw what have come to be known as the Four Passing Sights. Peering out from his carriage, he saw an elderly man, a sickly man, a corpse on its way to burial, and a holy man. That last figure possessed a certain quality of equanimity that Siddhartha admired.

This brief trip had a lasting effect on a willing mind. At 29, Siddhartha understood that all he had lived and dreamed until now was based on a pleasant illusion. In other words, there were difficult inevitabilities and sufferings in life from which wealth and power could not protect. He realized that no matter what manner of man or woman, all are open to trials and tribulations and all are destined for the grave. Siddhartha now knew this as a profound truth. Like you and me, he wanted to figure out how to get along in the world and to find some answers. In what would come to be known as the Great Going Forth, Siddhartha exchanged his jewels and robes for rags and traded in his sated desires for a hunger for deeper knowledge. In other words, he left.

But where could a spiritual newbie turn for answers to the difficult questions now plaguing his mind? In Siddhartha's day, it was common practice for seekers to find spiritual teachers, or gurus. And there were many available. In a sense, Siddhartha went shopping to find teachers willing to share their paths to true peace. He had tried luxury, but found it wanting. He adopted practices of renunciation and philosophical discussion, but to no avail. He tried self-denial to a point near death, but found no lasting answers. None of these could solve the riddles of death, suffering, disease, and poverty. None of these pursuits, as he had experienced them, could bring him to a lasting sense of self beyond the appearance of experience.

Many teachers (experts?) professed to have many answers. But these answers often did not agree. Imagine schools of thought sprouting up along the Indian river, Ganges, where gurus acted as headmasters and instructors claiming to hold metaphysical keys to the locked gates of wisdom. "Enter my school and discover the everlasting truths," they might have said. He tried. And he was locked out.

It's frustrating when you have a problem and the guidance you receive doesn't seem to fit. I remember going to my internist years ago to talk about a health issue. The doctor read my numbers and told me that I should consider one of the many available medical interventions that could get me to a place called "normal." I decided to go to a prominent institute to have further tests run. The head of this famous institute treated me famously. At the end of the visit, he didn't mention prescriptions or other medical procedures. He simply said, "Young man, your numbers look fine. Your problem is stress. If you have ways to reduce stress in your life, do them. Keep doing what works." And there you have it—the great Delphic oracle[3] reared its head. One set of numbers and two views. Two paths. What did I do? I headed down a road in between. I respected both physicians, listened to their expertise, and decided the truth had to lie somewhere in the middle. I honored all of their professional wisdom and my own feelings on the subject. I started a program of more intensive exercise, dedicated more time to meditative pursuits, and researched dietary approaches to help me along.[4]

I certainly would not recommend you do the same without consulting your own doctor (see my note). However, I would recommend that when you encounter a problem, go to the well-respected folks in your life and see what they have to say. Hear them out, ask questions, and weigh the issues. Then do what fits best for your situation. And yes, in the end, you may have to take a path that you would not normally choose or prefer, but at least you have well-informed answers and a good reason for having a procedure, eating bran, or buying that treadmill you don't have room for in the house. After all, when you have a reason for something and a helpful dialogue, it is easier to take appropriate action. But then again, reasons are often not enough. We need a *good* reason to do something.

And that is the path Siddhartha trod. He had a question and he wanted a good answer. He had lived a life of luxury and found it unsatisfying. He visited the holy men and learned at their feet. He received diagnoses and advice but still found it wanting. Eventually, after taking it all in, he decided to fashion his own method known as the Middle Way.

Finding the Sweet Spot

What is a middle way? You know, moderation—that word you love to hate. It's that thing we all think we support until it comes to chocolate or golf. It was on this path of moderation where Siddhartha finally found solid footing. It wasn't a way that encouraged only wealth, and it didn't mean starving himself until he could play a tune on his ribs with a mallet.

With this comfortable idea of a middle road, a desperately hungry Siddhartha took in some food, went to a tree, and sat down. But he didn't just sit. He sat in quiet contemplation with a resolve to stay put until he had insight into his questions. We don't know how long he sat, but it doesn't really matter. Then again, maybe I'm just saying it doesn't matter because I have trouble sitting still for more than a few minutes. But *he* sat. And as he sat, it is said that the temptations of the world came upon him. Some say a spirit of evil, Mara, tempted Siddhartha with earthly delights. But in the end, Siddhartha resisted and emerged victorious. He claimed to have gained insight into his past lives, *karma* (the cosmic law of cause and effect), and the way to release oneself from the bonds of suffering. In other words, he had attained enlightenment through moderation, patience, and diligence. When he stood from that spot, carrying his new knowledge within, he was no longer the same Siddhartha. He had a new mantle upon him. He had become the Buddha, or one who has awakened.

Whenever I get to this part of the Buddha's story—where he penetrates the illusions of life and awakens—it reminds me of dreams. At night, in bed, my mind is full of ideas, pictures, and bizarre worlds carelessly splattered on the canvas of the mind. But when the alarm sounds, those pictures disappear in a cloud of smoke. I am back in my room, in my bed, under the covers. I am back in what I perceive to be "real." Now, in my dream, I would swear to you that the two-headed monster coming for my winning lottery ticket while I stand frozen in my boxer shorts is real. He must be, right? I'm looking right at him. I even know about his life. The monster owns a convenience store and I'm in there talking to him about politics while he sells me a million-dollar-winning scratch-off lottery ticket that he now wants back so that he can retire with his monster wife of eighty-nine years that he married on a farm at age twelve.

It's real, right? Wrong.

It's merely an illusion. A play of the mind. It was what was real until something else came to take its place. It was sensible madness in a dream world without reason, just before reason's alarm beeped its awakening beep and carried me from that monster's store to my own room. I suppose we can also doubt the reality of my room and the alarm clock, but that's another chapter or, perhaps, another book.

Let's Get Really Real, Then We'll Lecture the Deer!

That inane story of one of my ridiculous dreams is an analogy to Buddha's amazing journey. Obvious, right? He achieved an enlightenment that allowed him to peer through the veils of dream and cloud, straight into the heart of reality. In a sense, he became a spiritual alarm clock. He made it the mission of his life to teach others about the *real* and to help them escape the bonds of their own prisons of illusion—to awaken us from our slumber to the reality of suffering and the ways to escape. Go ahead and give the dream monster the winning lotto ticket. It's just money after all. It's just an illusion anyway.

The Buddha's path was great! It was exciting! It was groundbreaking! It wasn't exactly popular right out of the gate.

After Buddha's enlightenment, his first stop was a deer park in Sarnath, India. There, he met some former pals with whom he had studied. They had parted from him when he decided he didn't agree with the teachings they were following together from one guru or another. But still, bros are bros in the religious world, and they listened to what he had to say. Buddha preached his first sermon to them, revealing the path to awakening. And guess what? They heard. And they became his very first students (the men, not the deer). I'm sure the deer got something out of it, too. I think they may even still be in the park, but I can't be certain. I don't live there. If you are ever in Sarnath and get to see them, tell them I say hi.

Buddha lived his own version of the good life until age 80, when he ate some bad pork offered by a faithful follower. Other accounts suggest his death was due to a particularly nasty mushroom or natural causes, but we'll probably never know. Anyway, just before Buddha departed, he instructed his closest disciples not to grieve. Instead, he taught non-attachment to the temptations of illusion even until the end. He beseeched his students to let him go in peace, trust their inner wisdom, and turn to their own paths. He told them they could burn bright enough in their missions to light their own ways forward. After that, he assumed a reclining position and died.

In the version of events I have presented here (again, there are others), there is no godly figure watching lovingly over Siddhartha. His mission is one of intense searching, personal testing, reason, and peaceful release. In the end, he is not ushered away into a heaven where others will follow if they believe in him. Instead, there is an extinguishing. There is the blowing out of the candle of karma. There is a legacy and roadmap left to others—a map one can follow with the light of his or her very own being. Anyone can achieve release on his or her own, in his or her own time.[5] Even my dream-monster friend.

Does Buddha's story relax you, or does it leave you wanting? Is this a path on which you'd feel comfortable? Do you like the idea of lighting your own way, or do you prefer another to flip on your switch? How you answer these questions is not a reflection on you as a person or as a spirit. It is merely an indication of what methods might work best for you as you try to work out your path through this world. And even if the Buddha's path is not for you, there are some interesting things we can all take away from his core teachings.

I will not insult Buddhism (or any other religious or spiritual pathway in this book) by claiming that each and every principle can be distilled into a few pages. That would be ridiculous. Instead, I am going to present a few points of interest on a scenic drive that would take many lifetimes to truly see in all its glory.

Permanent Change

The Buddha taught that we should not become overly attached to the things of the world. In other words, do not seek anything that is lasting or real in the material world. For example, when I awoke from the monster-convenience-store-lottery-ticket-boxer-shorts-married-at-twelve dream to my own room in a warm, comfortable bed in a solid space, I could not rely on those perceived realities either. The warmth under the covers would soon yield to the cold shower. A stuffy tie and tight shoes would soon replace the comfort of the bed. Even physics suggests that my solid walls are mostly empty space. (A note to physicists: if you have a quibble with anything in this book, please don't attack me. Instead, help us figure out what came before the big bang. Or give us insight into the gravitational forces in effect that always draw jelly bread to white carpet.) Therefore, if I am the kind of person who wanders the material world seeking anything solid, permanent, or wonderfully lasting, I will be bitterly disappointed. All I will find is change, and I don't mean the good kind in the cushions you can use to buy bubble gum. I'll find the other kind. The scary kind. The kind that makes sure my expectations and goals are not always where I left them, much like my keys or the remote (check those cushions). If I cling to a belief in, or a need for, permanence in a world that is constantly changing, what will I have then?

Well? What will I have? I'll wait.

Exactly! I will have empty hands and a lot of frustration. Or fear. Or lust. Or rage. To put it bluntly, if I cling to the things of the world with the idea that they will bring any lasting satisfaction, I will suffer. And that will suck. As I come to gain, I will eventually lose, and then I will seek to gain more. It's a terrible cycle.

By the way, I know what you're doing now. You're coming up with a mental list of things about you and your life that don't change. But if you think you have anything that lasts, think again. We are happy one day and sad the next. Coors men on Friday, while Saturday brings Miller time! Choose paint color in the store and then put it on your wall. Do you still like it? Remember the person that was so gentle and kind while you dated? Now that you're married, are they the same person all the time without fail? Are you? Are you always pleasant to be around? If no, then what happened? Do you wear every article of clothing in your closet with the same good feelings as when you first bought it? Do shoes from a year ago still make you as insanely happy as they did when worn at that first fundraiser? Do you consider moving from your country of origin during each election season? Have you ever uttered the phrase, "I wish I could go back in time! If I could, I'd..."? Go ahead. Be the same all the time. I dare you. Oh, and make sure to tell your hair, fingernails, body cells, and thoughts that you don't want to change. I'm sure they'll oblige.

Change is that place where we are not always comfortable. We pay a lot of lip service to the idea that we are good with change, and we claim that we are at peace with it, but when difficult changes happen, what then? Well, we often change our opinion of change. We may agree that change on a small scale is fine, but where is the line?

During my tenure counseling folks dealing with mental health and addiction issues, my agency needed to shift therapy schedules.

That didn't sit too well with many of my clients. I can't begin to tell you how many times the phrase, "Listen folks, life is change!" slipped past my lips. I had to stop myself from uttering that cliché, as it eventually lost all meaning. Instead, I turned to the Buddha—one of the world's first great counselors. I engaged complaining clients (and some coworkers) in discussions around the play of life and how things come and go all too regularly. That form of dialogue helped contextualize the idea that changing a meeting time or adjusting a form of therapy was yet another in a string of shifts that life could present. My clients often told me that major life changes or unexpected crises led to their depression, anxiety, initial drug use, or recurring relapses. Well, what better way to strengthen a life in health, recovery, or any other worthy cause than learning to manage change? In that regard, then, getting on good terms with change can help one shift from a life of drugs to a life of sobriety, or perhaps a change from perpetual anxiety to a little calm. It's not a cure-all, but my goodness, if we are a little more flexible, maybe we'll break less often. That goes for all of us, by the way.

Then again, it isn't always change we resist. Sometimes it's adjustment. Many of us say we want to make changes and that we'd welcome a nice detour, but when it comes right down to it, we don't want to make the adjustments necessary to bring that change smoothly into our lives. Or we use change as an excuse to dig in our heels where we are or cling to old patterns of behavior. In the example of addiction counseling, group time changes are sometimes met with a variety of this protest: "If you're just gonna change the times of group, then forget it. I won't come. I might as well stay home and relapse since I won't be able to get to group on time!" At this point, a counselor can engage in a discussion of the pros and cons of the necessary adjustments to a life in recovery and sobriety. Since life is change, and group therapy time is changing, and many clients are court-mandated to attend treatment to make a life change, they don't have very many options. They either make an adjustment or they don't. There are consequences to all choices (such as jail time for failing to attend group), and these consequences don't necessarily flow directly from the change itself, but from our ability or inability to adjust. If you are looking for an excuse to go back to old behaviors, you'll always find one, even if it means simply failing to adjust to change.

How about a more mundane example that is probably a bit closer to home? Years ago, my family took a trip to the American West. We loaded up the van and set off on our adventure. Being Easterners, we weren't schooled in the ways of sun and hot weather. At a monument in Colorado called Mesa Verde, we toured in excessive heat all day without sufficient fluids.[6] That night, my brother and I came down with hellacious cases of heat stroke. It was so bad, we had to park ourselves in an unplanned town at a motel for a few days until we could stand up (or crawl) without vomiting. Mom, Dad, and the grandparents pulled together and catered to us kids until we were well enough to move on. We didn't plan for this itinerary change, but illness—the greatest game-changer other than death—came upon us suddenly. It was at that point we needed to adjust as a family for a larger goal. It was still vacation, with just a little more time spent on the bathroom floor. Once we were all healthy, we climbed (slowly) back in the van and finished an amazing tour of a beautiful part of the United States. We have a family story and a good life lesson that we heed to this day.

Are you good with change? Can you adjust? Before you answer, consider: have you ever had a trip like the one just described—a trip that went awry? Maybe your spouse books the early morning tickets even though you're normally not someone who knows what five in the morning looks like. Fine. You adjust. Then, at the airport, your seats get screwed up. You think, okay, I'll take a middle seat. No biggie. Easy adjustment, right? You'll still get to paradise. You've got the hang of this adjusting thing! Oh, but then the flight is delayed. No problem, right? Then it's canceled. How are you with change now? Are you still okay adjusting to all of this? Are you still in a vacation mentality? When the room has one double bed instead of two queens, are you in a good frame of mind? When the hotel pool is drained, the rental car is smaller, or the rain pours down in the tropics, do you maintain an even mind? Was a vacation only vacation if it all went according to the itinerary and didn't change? Are you only a saint when you don't have to be around sinners?

The point is, no matter how well laid the plans and no matter how set the route, change is inevitable. We know this. I'm not telling you anything you haven't heard or experienced 43,209 times, give or take. The Buddha's point was that if you don't accept the simple fact of change and adjust to it instead of clinging to your ideas about how things should be, you will suffer. You will constantly be knocked off balance and will become a person no one wants to be around. You know that guy—he's the one that takes every empty seat next to where you are.

The Four Noble (Yet Still Harsh) Truths

What does any of this talk about change, adjustment, identity, and some crazy vacation where the author of this book and his brother toured a bathroom floor have to do with anything at all important? That's a good question. I think it's all about getting situated in the reality of our lives instead of the expectations. I've come to realize that Buddha's ideas aren't about building a house so much as learning to live in it. I remember when my folks moved from my childhood home to another house miles away. I spent a night in the guest room in the new place. My brother called and asked, "So? How is it?" I laughed and told him about the new house smell—the new carpets and freshly painted walls. There were new sounds outside and new toilets that, unfortunately, adhered to a low-flush technology. I replied, "It's nice, but it's not *home*."

Was I right? Yes and no. It was certainly a house by all definitions. There were doors and a garage. There was a patio out back and a nice view. There was gravel, some trees, and an unfriendly dog up the street. It had all the necessary trappings of household. But it took time before the family felt at home in the building. A house is something we build. A home is something we grow into after time and attachment set in. House is a mortgage. Home is an investment.

Buddha's teachings, as far as I can tell, are about learning to get comfortable with changes in our house. Learning to invest. They are about creating an understanding of and tolerance for the often-bland constructions of our lives so that we feel more at ease, more contented, and more at home in the world of change as we try to reach equanimity in it. When I examine a spiritual, religious, or philosophical teaching, I check it against how it makes me feel. I hold it up to my emotion meters to see if it makes me feel more or less at peace. In other words, does it make me feel more at ease about my place in the world? In that sense, the Buddha's Four Noble Truths make me feel comfortable, if not a little frightened. I find them to be revealing and useful—a great aid when I feel out of place in the world, or when I am just plain done with all the change and suffering we've just discussed.

But what are these truths that are so noble? The first time I encountered them, I thought, *my goodness, Truths? That's a tall order.* But then I got more intimate with them. Sit down here in my home and take a look with me. What do you think?

1 *Truth number one: Life is suffering.* The Buddha cuts right though the crapola, doesn't he? But hold on a second. Does "suffering" mean what we think it means at first blush? We've used it a few times in the chapter and sort of assumed a meaning. But I'm going to be bold and go out on a limb and say that no, it doesn't mean what we think it does right out of the gate.

How do I know?

I've met some Buddhists and they are among the friendliest and happiest people I've encountered. There must be more to the puzzle. And luckily, there is. I believe the Buddha is telling us there's a reality to being born into this world house—we are going to need to adjust to the fact that it isn't all we think it is. There is going to be disease, death, and disappointment along the way, and we aren't always going to get what we want, just like the Rolling Stones said. Not everyone is going to like us. Some soufflés will collapse and some egos will inflate. The kids will act contrary to our very detailed and precise parenting instructions, and sometimes elderly folks will not thank us for holding the door for them. Tough. That's life. It's filled with things that don't jive with expectation. The importance of this reminder is that once we know this to be the case, we can set about finding ways to deal with it. We can settle in with it. And that's good! Sometimes giving up expectation and giving in to change can bring great gifts, if only we'd bend to change's will instead of clinging to our own.

Still not convinced? Consider this: a friend of mine had prostate cancer. A pre-surgery x-ray accidentally showed too much of his body in a particular view. In other words, due to a small miscalculation, there was a change in the x-ray perspective the radiologist wasn't expecting. And guess what? The doctors found one of my friend's kidneys had a mass that would never have been detected otherwise. If this hadn't happened, how would his surgeon have known the kidney had to come out as well? Unexpected change can bring blessings. It's only when we don't allow for it that we suffer. Life is suffering. Life is change. Deal with it. Take it for what it is, and adjust.

Truth number two: We suffer because we desire things. This truth sucks. It sucks big time. It's the kind of sucking that makes me think of slurping on a lemon dipped in vinegar. All due respect to the Buddha.

I think the reason this truth is hard to swallow, much like that lemon juice, is because it is a painful reminder that my suffering starts with me—me and my desires and expectations. If I expect people to act in a certain way towards me, then I am bound to feel cheated and hurt when they don't live up to my standards. Or say I desire a certain car, but I don't make enough money to buy it. I might come to believe that I have somehow failed in life or that I am an unworthy person whose job isn't as good as someone else's.

If you find yourself scoffing at these examples, it may not be because they are wrong. It may be because they quietly infect a life in ways we find hard to admit. We're so used to locating the reasons for disappointment outside of ourselves, that for someone to suggest we are the reason we suffer is at best unappealing and, at worst, so traumatic that we block out all notions that it could possibly be true. You see, when we are forced to take responsibility for our own happiness from the inside, it means work. It means we must gain mastery over our own emotions. We must make the positive adjustment. Yuck.

When I was a younger man (am I old enough to use that phrase?), I had a head full of dreams. I wanted to do all sorts of things with my life, but wasn't sure I could. I didn't always feel like a self-esteemed success. Heck, I still don't. But when people heard about my goals and the difficulties I faced, some of them offered— quite without my asking by the way—to mentor me or help me. I felt happy. I felt excited. My initial angst and feelings of low self-worth slowly transformed into feelings of excitement and antici-pation. Expectation. The idea that someone from the outside could transform my life was tantalizing. And guess what? One by one they fell away. Promises and commitments turned into excuses and disappearing acts. At first, I thought it had something to do with them. Maybe they were just flakes or irresponsible-type folks. Then I considered that maybe it had to do with me (alt-hough, to this day I am still convinced a few of them were flakes). Maybe I was a hack or just unworthy of their time and attention. I wrestled with these thoughts for a long time.

But in the end, I realized that my desire for help with a goal and my disappointment around the failure of others to provide it was eclipsing the goal itself. And then? I had to take it a step fur-ther. It wasn't about getting help or even getting the goal. It was about getting right with life and people as they came (and went). In other words, it was about getting the Buddha's third truth.

Truth number three: To end suffering, end desire. If living is suf-fering, and suffering comes from desire, then there is only one conclusion if we want lasting peace: we must somehow reign in our out-of-control desiring. Let's take an example that's close to home. My home.

I completed my first novel-length manuscript in my early thirties. It had seen many hours of work, more than one drop of sweat, many edits, and a few major rewrites. Mom read it and cried. Hand-picked (of course) family friends read it and raved. Even I had become quite enamored with it—dare I say, attached to it. The next step? Send it out to agents, of course. Now, for any of you that have walked the aspiring-novelist path, you know it is a road ripe for Buddhist principles. Why? It's all about desire and suffering, my friend.

I convinced myself that the book's worth was somehow con-nected to how the literary community would respond. So I busily set about preparing query after query. I sent them out in waves. Droves. Herds. There is an astonishing rush of the new—of expectations unbridled—when one sends a piece of his soul out to others for approval. After all, Mom cried at the end, right? Slowly but surely the rejections poured in, just like all the writing bloggers on the internet said they would. "What you have written shows promise, but unfortunately, is not right for us at this time," was a common line. Let me translate it for you as a nobody-in-particular author saw it at the time: "What you have written shows promise, but unfortunately, you are not a famous politician, sports personality, an author with three bestsellers, a vampire or werewolf enthusiast, or a celebrity." They never even requested to read it.

More rejections piled up, and just when I thought it was done, still more seeped through the cracks. And that's only counting the agents who replied! After a while, I began attaching so much significance to the rejections that I lost sight of the initial project. I didn't start writing from a desire to be rich and famous and to get approval. I started writing to say something, to get something out there, and to change something. None of that—I repeat none of that—had changed. All that had changed was that I started desiring something (an agent or publisher) so badly, I suffered because of it. What began as one guy's personal project to do something good became an all-consuming need that only led me down darker and darker paths.

Solution? Write another book. And another. And another. And write them without attachment. Write for the pure joy of writing. Write because it feels right to write in your very core. Right? Right. I had to let go of the expectation that something ought to happen with my creative projects. I had to be okay with what I created and what I was doing, and I had to let go of the idea that somehow others could make it better or worse with their approval or disapproval. I don't have control over the publishing community, but I sure do have control over how I respond. Let's call that last line Noble Truth Three and a Half.

Truth number four: An end to suffering is possible if one follows the Noble Eightfold Path. The Buddha could have left us in a state of limbo after number three. In some great cosmic kick to the gut across the millennia, he could have simply said that life is suffering, and we all just need to deal with it on our own. Thanks for calling. Bye-bye. Get a haircut, hippie. But he didn't. And I'm quite sure he never used the word "hippie." Instead, he left behind a road to freedom with eight steps—a path of wisdom, ethics, and meditation meant as a prescription for what ails us. In other words, it's the antidote for attachment and desire. It's a way to end suffering. Paying attention now? Good. So what are these steps?

Eight Exhausting Steps to Eternal Relaxation

1. *Right understanding.* To put it bluntly, shove the Noble Truths and the other assorted insights into your skull. Understand that life will change. Understand that no matter how hard you try, nothing will stay the same. Know that the more you cling to things and expectations, the more you are doomed to suffer. Understand?

2. *Right intention.* Put a good energy out there, and don't harm folks. Practice lovingkindness. Put a good motive into what you do. Do good to do good, not to seek a shower of praise, accolades, or money. Commit to do good, be good, and to refrain from hurting others. If you slip up and do hurt someone, don't *mean* to do it. Good? Good.

3. *Right speech.* Don't tell tall tales or make other people feel two inches tall. Be an honest Joe or Josephine. Build folks up whenever you can. Use strong words to lift people up, not to

knock them over like bowling pins. If you need to correct someone, then do it gently. After all, you've screwed up zillions of times. Ease up on others.

4. *Right action.* Basically, go back to grade school and review what you learned there. Don't steal someone else's stuff, and don't draw on their drawings. Don't put your sticky hands all over someone else's clean shirt. Be kind to animals. Next, move on to middle and high school. Don't bully other kids because their pants aren't rolled right and they can't skateboard and they are kinda nerdy and…wait…sorry, that was my middle school (high school wasn't so bad). Now, get to college and beyond. Don't sleep around on your significant other, don't embezzle money, and don't claim to be something or somebody you're not. I'm sure that last one would have been in there if the Buddha had lived in a time of online dating.

5. *Right livelihood.* When you go to work, don't harm others. Don't do things to make a buck that rob people of their money or dignity. Remember that whole Weltschmerz thing at the start of this book? Don't add to it during regular business hours. Do whatever you want when your shift is over.

6. *Right effort.* Always search for positive ways to use your doing-ness, and do so in balance and clarity. Find ways to weed out your more…unpleasant qualities. Can you make an improvement anywhere in your life? If so, then focus. Work at it in good mind and through good doings. Make the effort.

7. *Right mindfulness.* Become aware of your body and mental states right here in this moment. Is that a cricket you hear? How does your breath move? This moment. These things. Observe. Watch yourself closely. Become a student of you. Cultivate an awareness of thoughts and feelings that normally tend to get out of control and work to control them. Don't become a reckless bull

in some metaphysical china shop, creating chaos and havoc because you can't keep yourself in check. Breathe. Mind what's happening. Commit to control yourself.

8. *Right concentration.* Remember all that stuff in number seven? Did it calm you? If not, don't worry. I've been working on it for over 20 years, and I still can't unclutter my mind for more than five seconds. Nonetheless, become aware of who you are and what you do, and then *concentrate.* Meditate. Focus your energy. Attain your bliss.

The Noble Eightfold Nobody

That all sounds like a whole helluva lot of work, doesn't it? I mean, we're just regular people in the world. We can't do all of that. But then again, maybe we can. Maybe we do! Let's look again at that fourth step of right action. I used a school metaphor on purpose to remind us all that we have been cultivating this right and noble pathway for a while. That schooling example is not only for step four in this random book you're reading, but a way of thinking about a lifetime.

We may not break our individual lives and deeds down into eight distinct steps, but we have been doing many of these things in life's classroom for a long time. Or, even if we haven't done them exactly, we've heard of them. Let me give you the digested version that I came up with during my exploration—the version that showed me that I, like you, have been on this eightfold path for years.

1. *Nobody's right understanding:* Life changes. Sorry.

2. *Nobody's right intention:* I screwed up. But I've learned from it. I must become a better person. Today.

3. *Nobody's right speech:* Yes [insert name here], you made a mistake, and it came at my expense. But you know what? You're a

good person, and I have faith that you'll get it right next time. That's the goal of life! It's okay. We're still friends.

4. *Nobody's right action*: Let me help you with those heavy groceries, ma'am. No thanks, I don't want a tip. (I used to be a bag boy.)

5. *Nobody's right work*: Are you feeling depressed today? Come into my office and talk. This email can wait.

6. *Nobody's right effort*: Wow, I can't believe I said that. I really need to watch my tongue. I'll try to be more conscious of my speech so that it doesn't happen again.

7. *Nobody's right mindfulness*: It's so good to be here. Now. Wherever I am.

8. *Nobody's right concentration*: Calm down. Take a minute. Breathe. There. Much better.

This eight-step path and all the other Buddhist principles in this chapter are much more involved and complicated than the versions I've presented here. You could spend a lifetime studying and mastering it all. But the point is, you've got a great start. You already know how to do these things. You've been doing them your whole life. You know things change. You know that when you want something you can't have, you suffer. You know how to be good and kind. You know. And I know you know, y'know?

So now, the only question is, do you have the courage to admit that you know? Can you take responsibility and start to do something about it? Can you adjust? What's the smallest step you can take right now to set your feet consciously upon the Buddha's path?

Book of Buddha Meditation

May change come on its schedule, and may I comfortably adjust in my time. Let my understanding of suffering and desire take me out of the role of victim and place me into the position of power—the power to shift perception from false to real through discipline, deed, and meditation. And if that doesn't work, do me a favor and just ease up on the suffering already!

NOBODY'S EXERCISES

1. The Greek Philosopher Heraclitus once said, "You can't step into the same river twice." What does this phrase mean to you? How do you adjust to change in your life?

2. The Buddha tells us that to live is to suffer, but as we have seen, that doesn't exactly mean what we think it does at first blush. Can you define "suffering" and identify ways that you have suffered and handled suffering in life merely in your regular course of living?

3. Fill in the prompts below with one action you do that follows a Nobody's Eightfold Path.

   Nobody's right understanding:

Nobody's right intention:

Nobody's right speech:

Nobody's right action:

Nobody's right work:

Nobody's right effort:

Nobody's right mindfulness:

Nobody's right concentration:

4. When you examine the Noble Eightfold Path, are there any areas that stand out to you as places you could improve? If so, write them below. Then, write a small step you can take today to set your feet back on the path.

5. Fill in the blanks below with thoughts on these prompts:

   I know I can deal with change in more positive ways because I:

   I can end a bit of life's suffering today if I:

   Your own meditation:

The Book of Moses

Forty Years, Ten Rules, and Two Stones

When I was about seven, and much shorter than I am now, I had a friend whose home was decorated in the remains of poor, defenseless animals that this kid's dad would shoot, stuff, and mount all over the place. He'd go on these expeditions and come back with this stuff. The worst piece in the house was a table made from four elephant feet. I don't remember ever meeting my friend's father, but even at such a young, tender age of innocence and universal love, I knew I loathed him.

One day this kid was over at my house, and we decided to go on an expedition of our own. I was chosen to lead our small band of three (my brother was there, too) into some woods out back. It was a simpler time when kids could go out to play, even in creepy woods, and parents didn't get a complex. Remember those days? They died out roughly the same time as disco. Anyway, I led us on a path to a clearing in the heart of the woods where we took a break and had a small snack. Then, we lined up in a neat row like good little scouts and I led us out on what I thought was the same path on which we came in. Nope. Within about twenty steps, we found our way blocked by prickly bushes of some sort and a patch of what appeared to be poison ivy. My brother wasted no time, of course, in cursing me as well as my terrible sense of direction. He was nine, you see, and knew all kinds of bad words that one picks up in fourth grade. By the time we arrived back at the house, exhausted and a little bloody, a vote was taken. By the slimmest margin of two to one, it was decided I would never again lead an expedition.

When I learned about Moses and his excursions through the desert, I was in awe. I couldn't even lead a 100-yard hike, but here was this guy who took folks on a 40-year journey. Of course, the thought isn't lost on me that, for all my detours, I eventually led us back to the house in under an hour while Moses took almost half a century, but still, I was envious. What a job Moses had! What an adventure!

A Little Bit About the Actual Bible

The ancient history of the Jewish people centers on stories of seemingly regular folks like you and me called into extraordinary action. We can read about their feats and journeys in the books of the Hebrew Bible, which is generally divided into three sections—Torah (the first five books of Genesis, Exodus, Leviticus, Numbers, and Deuteronomy), Prophets (including writings from Joshua, Isaiah, and Ezekiel), and other Writings (including Psalms, Proverbs, and Job). This collection presents the sacred narrative of a people and their origins. It is filled with colorful characters, love stories, competition, lust, anger, revenge, divine interventions, intrigue, and some good ol' fashioned prohibitions. Think of it like a high school yearbook.

The Torah is the part many of you probably know best. It is here where Adam and Eve, Noah, and Moses find their beginnings. Actually, it may be where *we* find our beginnings. Lots of popular stories and motifs fill its pages, including Creation, the Garden of Eden, and the Flood. Good stuff, right? I even capitalized them!

Whether you believe Biblical accounts are a 100 percent accurate recounting of ancient history or a fictitious collection of metaphorical morality tales, there is lots of entertainment in there. I suppose that's why the Gideons put one in your hotel room. In case you're bored and don't have cable on the tube, you have something to do. Although that may not be the best idea, because when I was a younger man on vacation with the family, I pulled the Bible from the hotel drawer and just happened upon Deuteronomy 23:1 which reads something like, "He that is wounded in the stones, or hath his privy member cut off, shall not enter into the congregation of the LORD."[1] Gee, that's nice. Considering a neighborhood ruffian had kneed me in the stones (yes, "stones" means what you think) a year earlier, imagine the effect that had on me when I read it. But that's okay. With all the time I now had free from my duties in the congregation of the Lord, I took up a few sports and actually became pretty adept at them. But I digress.

When you engage the sacred histories, including the sacred history of the Jewish people, don't spend too much time laboring in the search for historical accuracy. Most religions pay folks to worry about stuff like that. The rest of us should just take the trip. Enjoy the hero's journey and see if there is anything to take away from it that might be of significance. The Hebrew Testament provides a lot that is useful, especially for this modern-day nobody in particular on a search for meaning, even if his wounded stones leave him waiting in the car in the parking lot of the congregation of the Lord.

Who's on First? He'll Have a Wife in a Second!

The Bible wastes no time. Right in the first verse is the beginning of the beginning. In fact, Genesis 1:1 says, "In the beginning God created the heavens and the earth." Wow! No mystery there, right? We know what this part of the Bible is about right from the off. It is going to be a story of God.[2] It's also going to deal with God's exploits in the universe. God is probably going to have a special interest in our little corner of the galaxy, and there is definitely going to be something big happening. By the time Genesis chapter 2 rolls around, God's already done with the world, and the first guy, Adam, arrives on the scene. Adam names the things that God made, and he tidies up around Eden just before Eve arrives. Good thing he cleaned up, right? You know how it goes from there. In typical human style, both Adam and Eve break some rule or another and find themselves pitched out by the end of Genesis 3. Steeeeeeeeerike one! Nice. The ballgame has hardly begun, and a human messed it up in, I donno, less than a handful of pages. By the time Genesis 4 barely gets started, we have the first murder, where Cain kills Abel. Terrific. There are only about four people on earth, and they're already killing each other. Steeeeeeeeerike two! Then, Genesis 7 sees everything on earth washed away in a flood. Steeeeeeeeerike three!

Goodness gracious. Struck out in seven straight chapters. I can see God-the-manager in the dugout, gnawing on sunflower seeds, giving the evil eye and shaking his head as each of these players trudges back to the bench. Here's how I imagine it, in fiction-writing style:

"What was *that?*" God eyed Adam as Adam bounded down the steps into the dugout. He popped a piece of bubble gum into his mouth before hurling his helmet against the wall in frustration—narrowly missing his son, Abel, who was quietly keeping stats.

"I'm sorry, Coach. I know you told me not to swing at that apple from the Tree of Knowledge, but I just couldn't help it. That snake really knows how to pitch!"

"That's okay, Adam," God spoketh (speaketh? Spaked?) in a much calmer tone, remembering a tip he learned from Buddha to count to ten when angered. "Cain's up next. I'm sure he'll do a better job. I know he's gonna *murder* a pitch...isn't that right, Abel?"

Luckily for humankind, it isn't the last of the ninth in the Book of Genesis. If it were, the Gideons would be leaving a leaflet in the drawer instead of a book. Nope. The ol' ballgame is just beginning. Are these baseball metaphors doing it for you? You'd think sports would have been created somewhere in those first six days, but I guess not. If they had been, Eve would have found herself doing all the work in Eden while Adam called the first pizza parlor to deliver him a pepperoni pie right to his sofa in front of the first television. Either that, or he would have asked God to create eight more guys so that they could join a local softball league. No, wait...that wouldn't work. Beer wasn't invented yet, so what would be the point of a men's softball league in Eden?

I'm Just a Nobody, God—I Can't Possibly Do That!

Since we're making a beeline in this chapter toward what could arguably be the most important contribution to Western ethics ever (I'll ruin the surprise: it's the Ten Commandments), I propose we do a thorough background/refresher in the events that led up to that contribution. In that spirit, let's continue on with a five-minute tour of the Torah up to that point—give or take a few minutes.

Where were we? Ah, yes. People getting into trouble from the dawn of Biblical history. Well, in Genesis 11 and 12, everyone catches a break. Abraham comes on the scene (known until chapter 17 as Abram). God uproots Abram from his home in Ur in modern Iraq and migrates him to Canaan where God says he will make of Abram a great nation. In chapter 17, God makes his covenant with the now-Abraham. God says he will take care of Abraham and his descendants in exchange for circumcision of all male

Pg. 237 Notes
See Note
#3

descendants of the nation (yikes!). This takes us to the story of Abraham and Isaac. You remember. Abraham has a son Ishmael by his wife Sarah's maid Hagar back in chapter 16.[3] However, Sarah becomes pregnant with Isaac in chapter 21 and demands that Abraham cast out Hagar and her son Ishmael from the home. Or tent. Or whatever they lived in. God then commands Abraham to offer his son Isaac as a sacrifice in chapter 22, and Abraham obliges. God stays Abraham's hand and a ram is sacrificed instead. From there, we hear tales of Isaac, his son Jacob, and Jacob's son Joseph. It is a remarkable and long history and well worth some study. Just not right here. Our minutes are ticking down.

Let's skip ahead a few Biblical pages and get into the second book of the Torah, Exodus. Over time, the Hebrew peoples come to populate the land of Egypt. They become so numerous that the ruler of Egypt, or Pharaoh, starts to get nervous. Exodus 1:10 finds trouble brewing, and by the end of the chapter, Pharaoh has decided to throw the sons of the Hebrews into the Nile, allowing the girls to live. I've seen some cable documentaries about what lives in the Nile, and I can't imagine that would be very nice. In Exodus 2, a daughter of Pharaoh finds the Hebrew baby Moses hidden in a basket along the banks of the Nile. I don't have time to explain how he got there, but he's there. Pharaoh's daughter takes him in as her son. But Moses grows up displeased that his people are enslaved. In a rage born from seeing the beating of a Hebrew slave, he kills an Egyptian slave driver. Pharaoh finds out and is bent on killing Moses, but Moses flees to the land of Midian and marries Zipporah.

By Exodus 3 (is this going too fast?), the Israelites have had enough of bondage in Egypt and they cry out to God who decides it is time for their liberation. God finds Moses, now quite content to be living anonymously, tending to his shepherding duties like a regular guy—nobody in particular, so to speak. This is the burning bush story you've all heard before. Maybe you've seen it in cartoon form or in the movie with Charlton Heston. God identifies himself and tells Moses (not Heston) of a special mission wherein Moses must return to Egypt to free the slaves. What a boon! What a mission!

Moses isn't biting.

Instead, Moses protests to God. And, in Exodus 3:11, Moses gets close to this nobody's heart when he asks, "Who am I, that I should go unto Pharaoh, and that I should bring forth the children of Israel out of Egypt?" STOP! Do you see this? Are you hearing this? The great Heston...sorry, Moses...questions God about a divinely inspired mission, wondering aloud how he could possibly be the person God wants for this job. Yes! This is the proof in the pudding, people. This is the evidence of who we are as regular folks and the great things of which we are capable. Maybe I should have made this the first chapter. Meh. Too late. Anyway, Moses tries every tactic to get out of this. He says no one will believe he's on a divine mission, he says he doesn't know what to say, he says he isn't an eloquent speaker, and I think there's something in there about a dentist appointment. Luckily for the Hebrews, God clears Moses's schedule. By Exodus 4:20, Moses is off again for Egypt.

Needless to say, Pharaoh is not receptive to Moses's pleas on behalf of the Hebrews. However, God was not pleased with Pharaoh's not being pleased, so God sent plagues that didn't please anyone. Frogs, boils, hail, locusts, and gnats—sounds like some parts of the country I've driven through in the summer—rained down upon Egypt until the last plague: the death of the first-born sons of Egypt. Luckily, the Hebrews learn via the Lord that their own sons will be spared if parents mark their homes with lamb's blood. In other words, God will pass over the houses of the Hebrews. By the way, that is the origin of the Jewish holiday of Passover. Eventually enough was enough. Pharaoh sent 'em all packing. Moses parts the Red Sea, the Egyptian pursuers are smashed in the waves, and thus began a 40-year journey through the brambles and poison ivy behind Moses's house and...sorry, that was my journey with my brother and the neighbor kid. The 40-year trek was the *Hebrews* in the desert, Moses leading the way.

Whew! I think we came in just under five minutes.

God and His Man Moses Lay Down the Law

It is in the desert where Moses receives explicit instructions and rules from God, including the Ten Commandments. Yep. You heard right. Direct from God to Moses. According to Exodus 32:16, the two tablets were the very work of God and written in God's handwriting. That's pretty official considering no attorney was present to draft, notarize, and bill for it. These tablets are the big enchilada. They seal the deal between God and the people. In other words, God is saying, "Do this stuff for me, and I'll do my stuff for you." That's not a direct quote, by the way.

The Hebrew Bible is filled with laws on animals, property rights, food, wounded stones, and other things, but it is these Ten Commandments in particular that have had a magnificently profound impact in the West. They came to a man, Moses, once living in obscurity, and to a people, the Hebrews, once oppressed. These commandments have found their way into the hearts and minds of societies worldwide. But what are they? Do you have them memorized? Yes? Let me list them right out of Exodus 20 just in case your memory is faulty. Following each is commentary intended to spark discussion, debate, and thought. You can take it, leave it, or skip it altogether as you see fit. It's your choice, as is everything in this book. Feel free to kill some time in the desert until we're finished. Just don't get Heston angry.

Commandment 1: "I am the LORD thy God...Thou shalt have no other gods before me." Essentially, the message here is that even if there are other gods lurking around (and it sure sounds from the wording that there are other such gods lurking around), then *this* God should be first and foremost. And he[4] makes a good point. After all, he did go through a lot of trouble getting these folks out of Egypt. The very least they could do is follow his lead for a while and give him his due.

Commandment 2: "Thou shalt not make unto thee any graven image, or any likeness of any thing that is in heaven above, or that is in the earth beneath, or that is in the water under the earth." This appears to be command and commentary together. Don't construct idols like other folks around the region. Don't make animated movies about Australian clown fish trapped in a dental office in Sydney. Oh, and don't make that golden calf thing you are going to make 12 chapters from now in Exodus 32. God then goes on to say that if the people do these things, they will be subject to the wrath of a jealous and punishing God—a God that not only punishes parents, but also children until the fourth generation (Exodus 20:5). Luckily most of us are past the fourth generation since Moses on the mountaintop, but still, that's pretty heavy stuff. Not to question God's math or anything, but I'd say the reason the counseling biz is booming is because God still has plenty to punish us with a gazillion generations later.

Commandment 3: "Thou shalt not take the name of the LORD thy God in vain; for the LORD will not hold him guiltless that taketh his name in vain." Wrongful use of the name? Hmm. Does this only mean cursing with God's name? I like to think this also applies to sports figures who, in post-game interviews, inevitably thank God for a victory, thus implying that God is somehow absent from the other team's locker room. Isn't that somewhat of a misuse? I understand it is about giving thanks, but implying that

God shows more favor for a championship-winning server than the player who failed to hit the ball back over the net seems a bit out of line.

Commandment 4: "Remember the sabbath[5] day, to keep it holy." God then goes on to say:

> Six days shalt thou labour, and do all thy work. But the seventh day is the sabbath of the LORD thy God; in it thou shalt not do any work, thou, nor thy son, nor thy daughter, thy manservant, nor thy maidservant, nor thy cattle, nor thy stranger that is within thy gates; for in six days the LORD made heaven and earth, the sea, and all that in them is, and rested the seventh day: wherefore the LORD blessed the sabbath day, and hallowed it.

I love this commandment. God is *commanding rest.* Even if you find yourself at the movies on Saturday or Sunday, you should not go to the office. Not bad, right? Also, it makes sense. If we are somehow in the image of God, and God himself rested on the seventh day, then it is natural he would want us to have that day as well. He even includes animals. Pretty sweet. I know a terrier somewhere in the world that is going to be most happy.

Commandment 5: "Honour thy father and thy mother." This is clear: be nice to mother and father. I like to think this also fits into a modern society where children may honor whatever people make up their family—traditional or non-traditional. And for children that end up in dysfunctional families (also read: all of us), well, they may honor their therapist.

Commandment 6: "Thou shalt not kill." There it is, clear as day. But wait, it says "murder" in some translations. Is there a difference? Perhaps. In the end, it seems to come down to motive. If you kill in self-defense, is that murder? Probably not. But if you walk in on your spouse and your neighbor in bed and slay them both, it probably is a form of murder. Which brings us to…

Commandment 7: "Thou shalt not commit adultery." Perhaps this one should come before the murder thing. Anyway, this commandment also seems pretty clear: don't cheat on the people you love. And if you do? Well, lock the door.

Commandment 8: "Thou shalt not steal." Basically, this says that you shall not steal. Did I miss anything? I think this includes tasting grapes at the supermarket. But what about taking sugar packets from a restaurant? Or how about asking the waiter to box up that first meal that wasn't made right so that you can take it home to your child who eats anything? Is that stealing or *chutzpah*? I'm pretty sure the commandments are silent on chutzpah. I'll have to check.

Commandment 9: "Thou shalt not bear false witness against thy neighbour." I know this has to do with perjury, testimony, false accusations, and other legal things, but I'm going to expand it to telling lies. This commandment makes me smile. Not because I don't think it's valuable (I do!), but because after going to law school, I realize that if society actually followed this commandment, law school would be cut from three arduous and confusing years to one possibly necessary and slightly less confusing semester. Often, people in our society—whether on the stand or on social media—make things up or leave facts out to shirk responsibility, confuse others for personal gain, or to win an argument. It's a sad but true commentary. It's also the not-so-noble underpinning of the current political system and many religious scandals. Did you hear me politicians and religious leaders involved in scandals? Twisting words and using empty rhetoric to sway emotions or shift blame for personal or political gain is just not cool. No one can reach verbal perfection, of course, but I think we can do better than words that are always imperfect.

Commandment 10: "Thou shalt not covet thy neighbor's house, thou shalt not covet thy neighbour's wife, nor his manservant, nor his maidservant, nor his ox, nor his ass, nor any thing that is thy neighbour's." This is one giant property rights checklist. Like it or not in retrospect, these were the big-ticket items of the ancient world. Your home was your castle, servants weren't cheap or necessarily easy to come by, and it was the animals that tilled the fields, fed the kids, were used as offerings, and showed your wealth. Apparently God was aware of property issues and wanted to leave no room for doubt. And he didn't. What, you expected something different? He's God after all. Sheesh!

Aren't Ten-Commandment Devotees Just Being Old Fashioned?

Many students and other folks I know casually in and about town look upon religion as something antiquated and not entirely appropriate for these modern times. There might be something to that on some level. But that point of view begs two of life's more intriguing questions: do people pay attention to these Ten Commandments anymore? And, is there anything in them worth keeping? Maybe some are still relevant. Maybe some aren't. If you look at the commandments, you see mention of coveting oxen. I'm not sure I can point to a specific example of oxen coveting. Although I admit, my animal husbandry days are well behind me...like in a past life. But I'm pretty sure there are probably places where coveting oxen, camels, and ferrets is quite common, so I'll give God a pass on that one. As for adultery? Well, we need look no further than the tabloids or celeb gossip pages to see that this goes on all the time in much of the Western world without lightning strikes. And people disrespect parents every day. Maybe it does us some good to have some guidance.

Let's go a step beyond the commandments and consider if other Biblical rules and regs are pertinent to our lives today. Should they be? Can we be religious *and* selective? Many of us tend to pick and choose the things in our life for convenience or what best suits us in the moment. But what if we claim we want to build societies on Biblical values, or we hold Biblical and religious values up as a guidepost in politics? Are we taking a true stand for religion or simply pandering for votes? If you're in for a Bible penny, are you in for a Biblical pound?

The Bible is filled with prohibitions beyond the essential ones that cover wounded stones. For example, Exodus 21:17 states that if a person curses his father or mother he should be put to death. As far as I know, kids in first grade who curse mom or dad for failing to put a pudding cup in the lunch pail don't die. Rather, they end up as reality television stars or shock DJs. Daytime talk shows make a living off this stuff. Exodus 23:9 talks about the non-oppression of strangers in the land, and Exodus 22:21 reminds the Hebrews not to "vex" strangers in their midst because the Hebrews were once strangers in Egypt. Leviticus, another book of the Torah, also weighs in on this subject at 19:34. Yet there are political candidates who claim to love this Biblical God but build entire platforms on just the opposite of these teachings. They say they are following the law of the land, but what about God's laws? Exodus 22:18 allows the killing of witches, but I know some New Age shops where self-proclaimed witches are alive, well, and helping individuals on their life paths as they work with white light for the benefit of the earth and all peoples. These are just a few examples. Are these rules just as important as the ten biggies? If we ignore some of these ancillary regulations, do we get a pass on the Ten Commandments as well? We can leave that last question to dangle for now.

When I examine and evaluate the Ten Commandments, I don't just view them as a crusty, dusty ethics leaflet. I try to penetrate the plain written word to see something deeper. Something more. Something for today. Think that's arrogant of me to go beyond what's there? Then ask yourself why we have seminaries, religious commentary, and religious studies. Ask yourself why your particular religious group's interpretations are often so different from your neighbor's. Ask yourself why there are varying translations of the Bible and even different versions of the Ten Commandments. Let's keep the dialogue open.

My bet is that these commandments aren't always about the strict letter of the law, but perhaps are guidelines for a more orderly community. I'm not a gambling man, but I'd put chips down on the idea that these rules were given to us to interpret as we move through the world ages. I admit that it is sometimes dangerous to take any law or ethical code out of context and place it in a new one, and perhaps the Biblical codes are no exception. But what are we to do? If we don't seek to interpret or modernize, then how are we to grow as a civilization with religion and spirituality in our midst? We evolve and devolve as a society, not simply as individuals. Religion remains because it can change with us. These commandments are from a certain time and place and arise from its particular situation. Some are harsh and violent. I feel that doesn't negate them, but instead implores us to interpret them in our own time and place, with our very own special set of thrills, pills, ills, and wounded stones.

I'm guessing that even the most religious person in the Western world wouldn't murder his son for simple disrespect. And if he did? He would likely have to answer to a secular court system. Is that an example of changing with the times? Sure it is. Is everyone in agreement on this? Sure they aren't. Some groups may pine away for a return to Biblical days. But they can't do it in the modern West, anyway. And even if they could, they'd still have to pay taxes. The world has changed so much. Internet pornography, road rage, and supermarket grape tasting have brought new challenges for prohibitions on adultery, killing, and stealing. Do we do our forebears a disservice by not examining, interpreting, and, dare I say, evolving?

Should We Chuck 'Em Down Like Moses Did?

Exodus 32:19 presents the portrait of a Moses at the end of his rope. See, the people got tired of waiting for Moses to return from the mountain where he was communing with God. They wanted gods now. They wanted some reassurance. So what did they do? They melted their gold into a calf and worshipped it. When Moses eventually returns, and sees his people dancing around the idol, he gets miffed and throws God's tablets to the ground (I told you not to make that calf thing—I specifically warned you about that a few paragraphs back). New tablets were produced, but the damage was done. The people fell short. Don't miss that. Don't blow by that little snippet. I think it is important for us to know that even when God was clearly and demonstrably at the helm, people failed to see it and fell short. Imagine, then, how hard it is for us to be good in our imperfect world where God often seems so distant. So many false prophets come down from the mountain and demand our allegiance while we traipse around the idols of a material world. I know God's in the hotel drawer. But outside of that, it's hard to say where he is.

Today, our notions of perfection don't stem so much from the ethical people we know, but the celebrities we deify, the businesspeople we admire, and the politics we follow. In some ways, gossip columnists construct golden calves around which we dance. Crooked business schemes bilk people out of hard-earned money. Hollywood movies and modern notions of beauty serve up reasons for adultery day after day. We are surrounded by temptation, intolerance, addiction, stress, workaholism, indulgence, and greed on an incredible scale. So yes, these commandments may seem outdated, but perhaps they're a necessary guidepost ripe for new interpretations. Maybe they can be updated for our times. We will lose our way. We will fall short. We must strive on. Maybe the Ten Commandments can help.

Ten for Today

Let's try our experiment and see how these commandments are alive in everyday life, waiting to help us. We don't consciously follow all of them all the time anyway, so why not try to identify ways we do use them or could use them to improve things? Oh, and by the way, the usual rules apply. God can be any conception of god or gods you desire and, despite my little male-oriented convention in this chapter (calling god a "he"), god(s) can be male, female, or whatever mix you care to dream up. It can also be a web of energy. It can also be the Universe. Or, you can remove the word god from all of this and think about your obligation to your fellow humans. Do what you want. Just don't make a golden calf.

Nobody's Commandment 1: Have no other gods before me. Do you have an ultimate principle in your life that is supreme? Do you live your truth to the highest? I know you do. If you say you don't, then think about it for a minute. Perhaps your family comes first, no matter what. Maybe you are dedicated to helping others in need because you believe all people deserve compassion. Commit to the things in which you believe, but be receptive to compromise with others who may have different gods or goods. If you set your sights on worthy goals, then you are truly living this commandment. You are respecting your highest good (god).

Nobody's Commandment 2: Don't make idols. See Nobody's Commandment 1. Believe what you will, but don't judge a Hindu for his Shiva or a Catholic for his saints. Why? Because prejudices and biases become the true idols upon which we focus, while the spirit of humanity is lost. If you believe Jesus or Shiva or some form of Buddha is your highest conception of god, don't idolize it to the point where you can't hear someone else's position. Who knows? You may be speaking about the very same power even if your methods of worship are totally different. Not everyone's ancestors came from Israel, and not every Buddhist hails from Thailand. I'm sure you have plenty of friends who don't come from your neck of the woods, so just extend this thing you already do into the realm of the religious or spiritual. Then you will not only have love from your conception of a god, but you will also have the love and respect of your neighbors. Don't idolize negativity and division. Instead, put the love principle first.

Nobody's Commandment 3: Don't misuse God's name. This doesn't only mean keeping God's name out of swear words. A bar of soap to the mouth one time can do that. This commandment could refer to using God's name to devalue others or to claim superiority in competition. If the God of this chapter, the Creator God, brought everything into existence, then surely your individual home run is as worthy as the pitcher who threw the ball. Everything we do, no matter how seemingly ordinary, is an accomplishment in the sight of God, including going to the grocery store, raising a child as a single parent, picking up the kids from soccer practice, or ironing a shirt. Be respectful not only of your misuse of God's name, but how your praise of the name makes others feel. By all means, give thanks to God for all of your accomplishments, as they are all yours in the name of God. But remember, my accomplishments are worthy as well, even if they seem unimpressive or make your ventures seem more successful (I'm the pitcher who threw that home run ball). My son's missed soccer goal is every bit as valid as your daughter's goal save. They are both children of God.

Nobody's Commandment 4: Remember the sabbath day and keep it holy. You already know how to get some rest, so let's simply expand the idea. Thinking of going in to work on Saturday? Fine. But will you miss your son's piano recital? Do you have a report that absolutely must get done? That might be a reason to pick up an extra shift at the office. But if you're going in on the weekend simply to avoid a discussion with your spouse, that might not be so good. If you are busy on weekends, do you have a spiritual or meditative practice or space of rest during the week? I'm sure you do. Is it yoga? Prayer? An AA meeting? Corvette club? Man cave with video games? Don't just remember the sabbath. Remember to rest. Remember to take some time out. Remember your loved ones. Remember to give thanks. Remember your spirit.

Nobody's Commandment 5: Honor your mother and father. I know you sent your mother a Mother's Day card. See? You do this commandment already. But when was the last time you picked up the phone and gave her a call? Really? Well, don't you think it's time? If your father has departed this earth, have you given him a silent thought and a prayer? Don't know your parents? Then have you told your caregivers how much they mean to you? Perhaps you are in therapy because of a parent or lack of parental authority. Have you been totally honest with the counselor and yourself about your feelings in an earnest step toward healing? Have you told both sides of the family story? If there is truly only one side— yours—then how are you dealing with it so you can move on?

This commandment isn't about honoring parents through stone monuments (you know what's funny? I accidentally typed *"mom*ument") or naming hospital wings to honor the dead. It's about respecting our roots. I'm not suggesting you throw mother a parade with balloons and streamers. But maybe you could just wing off a kind email now and then. Or not. Your choice.

Nobody's Commandment 6: Don't kill. I have full confidence that you readers are clean on this one, unless you are on death row for killing and had someone bring this book to you. In that case, thank you for reading. But even if your conscience is as shiny as a new penny, are you praying for the wellbeing of folks in other countries who are oppressed even unto death? How does your vote affect foreign policy on these matters? Even if you are not in the Peace Corps or a living saint, you can still do small things to protect and heal others. Maybe "kill" includes apathy to killing as well.

Nobody's Commandment 7: Don't commit adultery. Texting (sexting), illicit emails, or going to another person with all your relationship woes while leaving your partner in the dark are all ways of committing adultery. At least, these are ways that I have heard about in the press, on TV, and from students and clients. Meaningful relationships involve real feelings, real togetherness, and real sex between people. If you find another person and want to stray, break off what you have now. Or think about why you want to stray. I'm not the morality police. Far from it (trust me!). I'm just suggesting courtesy in the relationship and in the bedroom. Is that too much to ask?

Nobody's Commandment 8: Don't steal. I'm sure you pay for your groceries. I know you teach your kids to be honest. That's all part of this. But how do you make your money? Do you suck people into money-making scams with the phrase, "This isn't a pyramid scheme"? Do you take credit for work that isn't yours to get ahead? Do you fudge the paperwork? Stealing is more than pocketing gum at the convenience store. It's a mentality that says it's okay to borrow things without asking, copy/paste an essay from the internet and hand it in to your instructor, or cheat on a test. No person is a total saint (well, maybe there are a few—I think we call them "saints"), but that doesn't mean we shouldn't at least try to be as honest as we can be. We want recognition for our accomplishments and a fair price for our time and effort. In that spirit, we should give others their due.

Nobody's Commandment 9: Don't bear false witness. Are you an attorney? If so, do you give fair and complete disclosure to the other side? Do you seek truth in court, or just a victory? What about the non-legal world? If you decide to take a stand on something and weigh in, do you give an honest and fair opinion? Are you a blame shifter? Do you tell yourself or others that someone else is "the problem" so that you don't have to change?

Yes, there are probably times when a small lie is better than a big mess, but has half-truth, hyperbole, or exaggeration become the norm for you? If you take on the responsibility of witnessing for or against a point of view, perhaps it's best to be less obtrusive, more cooperative, and a heckuva lot more reasonable.

Nobody's Commandment 10: Don't covet your neighbor's property. You share. You do! You have friends over for dinner, loan the neighbor your tools, and donate items to charity. You play nice with the things you have. But what about your outlook on what others have? Envy is the downfall of many a self-esteemed person. Are you ashamed to pull your clunker out of the garage in the morning while the guy next door revs his sports car's engine? Do you secretly want to steal your buddy's girl instead of searching for your own perfect mate? Coveting is not just something for Biblical times and oxen. Often, it's what keeps us blind to the blessings in our own life. There's certainly nothing wrong with wanting something more. The problems seem to start when all we want are more things to the detriment of the bounty we already have.

No matter what you think about the Ten Commandments, Judaism, Moses, or my wounded stones, you need to remember that you are living in a society—whether that's your home, your neighborhood, your town, or whatever—and societies are communal projects. Even if you don't like the rules in the Bible, I'm sure you still have personal rules and codes to help you along in your day. That's right. You already have commandments that help you get by. Recognize them, live them consciously, and make life sweeter for all of us.

Book of Moses Meditation

Let there be an ethical core to my being, and let me find the courage to lead others by example and not by mistake. Let me take on a task I fear, and lead me through the deserts of doubt to a positive result. If mine enemies seek to destroy me, lead me across the sea to safety. After that, please do that wave-crashing thing you did years ago in Egypt for Charlton Heston so that I can ensure mine enemies are really gone for good.

NOBODY'S EXERCISES

1. The Biblical history of Judaism is amazingly complex. But really, a lot happens in the Bible in just a few pages. Can you think of a time in your life where everything sort of happened at once and maybe overwhelmed you, yet you came out a better person?

2. God wiped out the corruptions of the earth with a massive flood, but he let new life spring forth. Is there something or someone in your life you need to wash away so you can move on?

3. Moses protested and protested when God asked him to return to Egypt on a special mission. In the end, Moses went. What is something you've been resisting that could be quite good for you?

4. Look back and consider your own family hist
   Complex? Somewhere in between? How d(
   matriarchs and patriarchs that came before)

5. I know you possess leadership qualities. You many not think
   so, but take another look. Where or when in your life have you
   displayed a knack for leading somebody (or a bunch of somebodies) to a goal?

6. Fill in the prompts below with actions you do or thoughts you
   have that create your personal Nobody's Ten Commandments:

   Nobody's Commandment 1 -- Have no other gods before me:

   Nobody's Commandment 2 -- You shall not make an idol:

   Nobody's Commandment 3 -- Don't misuse God's name:

   *Nobody's Commandment 4 -- Remember the sabbath day and keep
   it holy:*

obody's Commandment 5 -- Honor your mother and father:

Nobody's Commandment 6 -- You shall not kill:

Nobody's Commandment 7 -- You shall not commit adultery:

Nobody's Commandment 8 -- You shall not steal:

Nobody's Commandment 9 -- You shall not bear false witness:

Nobody's Commandment 10 -- You shall not covet your neighbor's property:

Your own meditation:

The Book of Confucius

Be a Man, but Know Your Place Among Men

I'm close with a set of twins. We have known each other for years, and their friendship has had a profound impact on my life. We met in high school, and I can remember spending a lot of time with them, watching their interactions. I was always fascinated at how similar and different they were (and still are!). Not better or worse. Just different. Unique. Over the years, I have watched these two grow, raise children, own homes, and interact with friends, and I note the subtle variations between them. In some ways, though, no matter how different they are, at their core they seem to carry a piece of the other.

When I reflect upon the world of religion, I see traditions that are in many ways similar, yet opposites. They may carry some parallel messages, but the trappings are quite different. Their histories diverge. Sometimes it's hard to see the shining, kindred cores. The twin sense is lost in the sea of time, history, diversity, and misunderstanding.

Let's keep that metaphor in mind as we examine the world of Chinese religious tradition. Specifically, Confucianism and Taoism. There is a linking symbol for both religions—the familiar spinning wheel of balance composed of twins. These aren't just any twins, but twins that contain in each the very heart of the other. I am speaking of the yin yang (see Fig. 2).

Figure 2 - Yin and yang

The first feature that should jump right out at you is the over-whelming sense of balance. There is nothing offensive to the eye. A simple circle is divided into two smooth, swirling fish that complement each other in stark black and white, creating an effect of equal relief. In other words, each side is necessary for the other to stand out. It's almost as if one were missing, the other might just ooze off into eternity.

The next striking feature is the small, opposite-colored dot contained in each side. Each portion of the figure contains a drop of the other deep in its core. In fact, it almost looks like an eye. In one way of thinking, this eye is what gives sight to the other direc-tion—a direction that would otherwise be blind to its twin. Re-member that the white side is not "good," and the black side is not "bad." There is a tendency to think of light and dark as staunch opposites (thanks for that, *Star Wars*). But that's not the case here. Instead, think balance. Think necessity. Think enhancement. Think chocolate and vanilla ice cream with deep, rich hot fudge and feathery, white whipped cream uniting them. Sweeter together. For the yin and yang, neither can exist, nor have sight, without the other. They form a complementary pair.

So, what does each side represent? The white portion is yang—light, heat, and action. It's the hot sauce at a raucous pizza parlor. It is a group of children roughhousing on a summer day. There is activity under the blazing sun and a feeling that something can be accomplished. It is often considered the masculine side of the circle. The black side is yin—dark, cool, and receptive. Yin represents the comfort of eating a juicy plum while reclining in the shade. It is the same children from above, now lazing under a late-autumn moon gazing at the stars. There is nothing to do or say. There is only to be. It is often considered the feminine side of the diagram.

The message of yin and yang is loud and clear: there is time for work and time for rest. A time for play and time for repose. We must taste the zest of life, yet tame the spicy fires to progress in harmony. Can you pinpoint a practical way this diagram functions in your life? Let me provide an example. Suppose you need to tell a friend that something they do bothers you—perhaps because it is destroying your relationship. Do you feel good about it? Are you excited to have that conversation? Probably not, unless they really, really deserve it! I don't know, maybe they hum while they eat or they asked out that person at the bar before you could. But no, usually a confrontation, even if well intentioned and necessary, engenders difficult emotions. Heated words. If we have the conversation, we will probably seek to reconcile soon after to repair any damage. The point is, when fiery (but necessary) words are spoken, cooling words may restore balance. And sometimes we find that we have a stronger relationship. We may find there is more bond or more trust. Necessary action is the complement to necessary repair.

Two members of the Chinese religious family, Confucianism and Taoism, are often considered yang and yin respectively—complementary and necessary elements in a robust system of beliefs that has endured for thousands of years. In this chapter, we will consider Confucianism, and in the next, Taoism.[1]

Confucius—A True Nobody's Somebody

Confucius, also known as K'ung-fu-tzu or Master Kong, was (probably) born to a noble family in 551 B.C.E. in the Chinese state of Lu. His father died when Confucius was very young, and he and his mother lived in poverty. Despite their monetary difficulties, she raised him up to be a gentleman and a scholar who enjoyed cultured hobbies such as archery and music.

Confucius sought a life in politics, but never attained a very high rank. His greatest legacy was as a teacher, and he is often referred to as the First Teacher. A study of the portrait of Confucius reveals a humble man who considered himself more a transmitter of wisdom from idyllic times in the past than a generator of new knowledge. I guess this would make Confucius a lot like many (but not all!) of our grandparents—believing that the cures for today's ills can be solved by hearkening to values of the past, all while criticizing computers and cell phones. And suggestive dance. And loud music. And uppity teenagers. And back talk. Or maybe that was just the plot to *Footloose*.

After Confucius's death in 479 B.C.E., philosophical schools,[2] including different flavors and variations of Confucian and Taoist thought, duked it out to gain favor in a China in turmoil. Back then, China was not the (relatively) unified country it is now. It was a patchwork of kingdoms with different rulers and different ways of ruling. Sort of like a Risk board. Remember Risk? I do. I always got my butt kicked. Boggle was more my speed. Anyway, this era of tumult from approximately 475 to 221 B.C.E. is known as the Warring States Period. Teachers and philosophers (a.k.a. political advisors—imagine how great it would be if political advisors today were teachers and scholars and not a bunch of corporate suits) bustled from court to court seeking to win favor for their particular ruling philosophies.

For a time, a rather harsh, legalistic school won favor among rulers. These folks believed that human nature is one of fundamental selfishness and idleness, and that strong punishment was the most effective way to keep people in line. Sounds like high school again, doesn't it? But as the years progressed, legalistic attitudes gave way to a softer Confucian ideal. People, Confucius thought, are not bad at heart, but need guidance and education rather than punishment and harshness. A man named Dong Zhongshu (179-104 B.C.E.) eventually convinced the elite that Confucian thought could unite China.

Be Super—But Know Your Place

What are some of these values that have had such a profound impact on China and scholars abroad? How could one man's recounting and transmitting of past wisdom have so much influence? My guess is that it has to do, yet again, with a nobody's favorite words: simple common sense. I'm not suggesting that Confucius was a simpleton. Quite the opposite. When I read about his life and point of view, I am struck by the powerful truths cloaked in elegant simplicity and a mind-boggling sensibility.

The problems in Confucius's China were many. Confucius believed that if one could restore social harmony, one could restore balance. For Confucius, then, the goals were twofold: create a society of excellent people, and foster harmony in that society. Idealism is a common theme in religion and spirituality. But as we all know, perfecting a self or perfecting a society is often a goal fraught with potential pitfalls—not the least of which is the fact that selves and societies don't always cooperate. In fact, selves and societies often whine, complain, and duck responsibility. If selves and societies throughout history could talk, they might say, "But it's not my fault! It's the other guy. After all, I'm doing my part. Why doesn't the other guy buck the hell up and pull his own damn weight around here? Am I right, other guy? Hello? Am I right?"

Consider this: my mom (and perhaps your mom) used to say, "Drive carefully!" before I left the house each morning. Then I would say, "I do drive carefully, Mom." The last words from her mouth as my car door slammed would be, "It's not you I'm worried about. I'm worried about the other crazy drivers on the road!"

Well, let's be honest. I am a careful driver, even though Mom's sentence construction seems to imply I was one of the crazy drivers. However, in my younger days, I did my share of dumb stuff (not any more, of course—at least at the time of this book's publication). But in my mind, I agreed with Mom. It was the other guy. I was driving just fine, right?

In a Confucian way of thinking, Mom's logic seems to pass muster. All people must take responsibility for their own strengths and weaknesses before and after they leave the garage. Even if you believe it really is the other guy that has the problem, you must recognize your part in the social fabric, honor your obligations, and serve not as a mouthpiece for blame, but an example of greatness for all to follow. You must be the world's hero. You must be the careful driver. Even if you think it's the other guy who has all the issues, you should keep on doing your part as best as you can. Strive to improve even your perfect habits. Yield to ramp traffic, stop on red, slow down on yellow, use a hands-free device, and brake for jaywalking pedestrians instead of speeding up to teach them a lesson about using crosswalks. Do your best to keep your oxcart on the muddy path. It's your responsibility to drive like a gentleman even in a world full of irresponsible louts. So, in essence, Mom was saying, "I know the other drivers are crazy out there! I'm just reminding you to be a good example to them all." I'm sure that advice would have gone over great with a teenager.

Setting the good example is the start of a great recipe that would carry China for a few thousand years. In the end, when it comes to being an individual in society, one must develop great qualities, know one's place, and be virtuous. If everyone follows that simple, logical formula, then society will be harmonious and accidents will decrease.

The Super You

Have you ever dreamed of an idyllic society where things run smoothly and there are abundant folks around who know the answers to life's most troubling questions? Or perhaps you pine away for the constant guidance of a social mentor who knows exactly what is expected in each situation and can keep you on the straight and narrow. Think of an interpersonal paradise where all your social needs are met. Do you ever wish there was a constant Yoda to your floundering Luke? What about a society where everyone is a Yoda? How does a world where everyone is a likely hero sound?

In a way, that was Confucius's idea. Imagine a person who has imbibed virtue and culture since youth, as eagerly as a mother's milk. He might be kind and compassionate, yet know when to correct. Perhaps she knows just the right custom in each setting and shows modesty in her dealings with others. Sensitivity and appropriate judgment abound for this person. Think of it as the exact opposite of Congress. The problem in reality is that these great and virtuous souls in our lives are often the folks we love to hate, if only because they threaten to remind us just how much work we have left to do on our own human-nature honey-do lists.

If you can imagine such a wonderful person (I can, and it's not me), then you might be imagining the *junzi*, or Confucius's ideal person. Perhaps you know someone like this. Or, as we said, perhaps you get annoyed with someone like this. Perhaps you look up to her as a guide and mentor. Perhaps you avoid him when you see him at the supermarket. Nevertheless, this may be that ideal person in your life who serves to further the Confucian dream: in a society where everyone strives to be exemplary, all serve as examples to others until a new norm is reached. A norm of excellence. But how do we learn to be this kind of person?

As I Said, Know Thy Place! Oh, and Know Thy Category.

Confucius, as you now know, taught the goods of social order and virtue. He believed that mastery and mindfulness of certain categories could lead to the ideal society. Since humans interact in social settings, the logic goes, if they know their hierarchical place in society, they will contribute to harmony. Know place, know peace. No place? No peace. For Confucius, harmony was wrapped in the warm blanket of Five Great Relationships. Let's examine them.

1. *Ruler/subject.* Some folks put this one first on the big list. Some folks put it last. I'm putting it first. When you read "ruler," think about your modern politicians and folks in the local town hall. Or do what I do and try to never think of these folks. Maybe if we stop thinking about them, they'll go away. Far away. Far, far away. Maybe they'll form their own colony on an island somewhere and leave the rest of us alone. I'm sure there are some good ones, but we'll be able to figure out who they are because the others will toss them out of the colony.

Anyway, for Confucians, it was essential that rulers see themselves as fatherly figures to the ruled. And doesn't that make sense? People look to their kings, princesses, presidents, and megalomaniac tyrants as parental figures in a way. Rulers hold the keys to the coffers and they set the rules, whether subjects like it or not. If rulers think of themselves as fathers, they might be more inclined to set a good example that will be followed in homes throughout the land. Mentor those whom you rule, and they will respect you and your authority to rule. Or else they'll send you to live on that island with the other politicians.

2. *Father/son.* See how this works? Following right on the heels of the politically modeled relationship of the home comes a relationship in the home. Fathers and sons were considered the bedrock family duo in an ancient Chinese society based on household structure. In modern times, we can think of this pairing as representing any parent-to-child relationship, especially considering the diversity of parenting and family styles. This category sees parents as responsible for molding a child's character, providing education, and giving guidance. Children should repay that kindness by providing for their parents in their parents' elderly years and being obedient.

Of course, in this modern age, there is often a disconnect. So many times in my social work days, a client sat with a box of tissues and told me that his or her mother or father is too involved in their personal life, forcing the client to a life of drugs or an emotional state of anxiety. But then again, so many tear-stained tissues came from clients whose parents were not involved enough—leading clients to a life of drugs or an emotional state of anxiety. These were all good people. Kind people. Sensible people. They just saw this relationship through different lenses. Confucius, help us!

3. *Older brother/younger brother.* In China, and probably in many Western households as well, the status of the eldest brother is important. Think of him like the surrogate father. When Dad (or, in modern times, Mom and Dad) isn't around, older brother is the de facto man of the hour. In this relationship, the older brother is a mentor and example, and the younger brother is a respectful and willing companion.

Take my older brother. Why, when Mom sent us off on the school bus for the first time, I was scared. I was crying. But wait! Never fear! Older brother was there to guide and help me. He was there to direct me. Actually, he got off the bus at the correct stop, but left me behind screaming and tripping in the aisle as the bus pulled away. But that's not the point. When he didn't have his mind distracted in such stunning fashion, he was an example for me. He still is. I just don't take the bus with him anymore.

4. *Husband/wife.* Dad goes out and slays the pig, and Mom cooks the bacon. In Confucian times, this was a relationship of duty and expectation in the house that would create harmony in the home. Perhaps in ancient times there was more talk of leadership on the husband's part and obedience on the wife's part. Today, in many households, traditional roles have reversed. Wives are taking care of duties once thought to be the domain of men. And that's great! "Yes, Dear" is now a gender-neutral way of keeping the peace. No matter which way the roles go in your home, respect is the key.

5. *Friend/friend.* Have you ever had a mentor or a favorite teacher? Did I ask that already? Maybe it was an older friend or someone at your job to whom you could go with your questions. These folks are often a good addition to our lives, as they are people who can get us back on track when we falter. For Confucius, this was an especially important relationship. I like to think of it as the cement that holds social bricks together. You may have a

caring family within the household, but when you are struggling in school or are lost in your career, it is a friend or mentor that can make it all good again. Perhaps they're just the person who buys you a drink when the husband/wife thing isn't going so well or when you're still bitter that your brother left you on the bus.

These roles are not just a bunch of randomly obvious categories. Yes, the naked eye can identify the pairings, but it is the sensitivity and wisdom with which we navigate them that makes all the difference. Confucius believed that if people knew their role and knew their place at every step along the way, then society would chug along nicely. Don't know what to do in X or Y situation? Check your list of roles, see where you fit, and do what is fitting in that role. In fact, this focus on knowing what to do in any situation takes us to the other great cornerstone of Confucian thought, the virtues.

When You Just Know, You Truly Know

If you wanted to be a Confucian gentleman or gentlewoman in the harmonious society, there were a few things that were expected in addition to knowing your role. There were some virtuous character traits to help you become the kind of person others wanted to be around, instead of just some troublemaker who wandered around the village making a mess of everyone's neat social order. I knew that guy in eighth grade, and trust me, he sucked. Anyway, I've selected five virtues from the vast array that have helped me. There are more, if you want to do your own investigation. But take a look at the ones I've listed, and see what you think.

1. *Ren*. In Chinese characters, this word is a blending of two things: "human" or "person" and the number two. Thus, it represents the way two humans should act toward one another. Think kindness. Think compassion. Think being considerate. Think the

opposite of election-year politics or the jerky person in the sports car who cuts you off on the freeway.

2. *Shu.* You know the Golden Rule, right? Say it with me: do unto others as you would have them do unto you. Good. Confucianism has a version, but it's a little different. Shu is often called the silver rule. In essence, it says: don't do to others what you don't want done to you. Do you see the difference? Read them again. One is a positive statement of action and kind deed, while the other is a statement of self-disciplined restraint and supreme empathy. See it now? No? Okay, say you are the kind of person who gets a sick and twisted thrill from jumping off a perfectly good boat into the water to scuba dive with sharks. Your friend, however, is afraid of the ocean. Would you buy him scuba lessons for his birthday? You wouldn't? Well, then you are doin' shu.

Shu asks you to consider the other person before you act, even if you are acting in a way you find reasonable or appropriate. You like making poor decisions by jumping off boats into shark-infested waters. Your friend likes keeping his limbs. Therefore, don't give the gift you would want given unto you. Instead, stand in the other guy's fins. If he likes them dry on the boat, buy him a beer and a fish dinner on the beach instead.

3. *Li.* Li is a wild little word that has many a translation. In this context, think of it as appropriate ritual or acting properly in social situations. If you see a solemn service taking place, don't yell out insults or mock it. That would make folks really unhappy. It'd tear up the fabric of orderly society. If you enter a home for a holiday, take care to observe where you should sit. For example, don't park yourself at the head of the table, unless invited. Seek guidance from someone if you are unsure how you should act. If there's one roll left in the basket, and you want it, restrain yourself and see if someone else would like it first. Are you a Christian at a Jewish ceremony? See what others are doing. Stand respectfully when

others do. Ask respectful questions. Take social cues. Become li in your actions and in your non-actions.

4. *Xiao.* This is filial piety. That's not a phrase we hear too often in our everyday lives, but it means to respect family (siblings, parents, elders, etc.) and ancestors. It means doing things they would expect or like you to do. Yes, it even means hugging that relative who always smells like mothballs.

5. *Wen.* If you love art and culture, you are living wen. This one doesn't appear on everyone's list, but, as a writer, I couldn't resist. It means getting acquainted with painting, music, and poetry. If you do what is right, are considerate, and can talk on a variety of cultured subjects, then you are kind *and* well-rounded. I sometimes struggle with this virtue. For example, I played trumpet for a year in fifth grade and hated it. Especially the spit valve. Does that count as wen?

The Nobody Gentleman and Gentlewoman

We've looked at yin and yang, Confucius's Five Great Relationships, and five assorted virtues. That's 12 different things! Ten Commandments were so much easier because there were two less things to keep track of, and they came on a neat and tidy set of tablets. But what does all of this mean? We can't possibly be what Confucius wanted us to be, right? It's too much work. Ah, but you know that I'm going to prove to you that we are already living, or know how to live, these Confucian ideals. We already know how to bring about balance for ourselves and others. We already know how to be good junzis and junzettes. I'll prove it through a Nobody's practical review of relationships and virtues.

1. *Nobody's ruler/subject:* This politician doesn't support educating our little ones, and I hate those ties he wears. Plus, I met him once, and he was not nice. I'm voting him out.

2. *Nobody's father/son*: Yes, Dad. Let me pause my video game. I'll be right there to take the trash out!

3. *Nobody's older sibling/younger sibling*: Tommy, give me your hand while Mom is in the store. I don't want you to get lost.

4. *Nobody's husband/wife*: I'll push my tee time back a few hours so that I can help you with that leaky sprinkler in the yard.

5. *Nobody's friend/friend*: Go home to your wife, John. I'll finish this report for the meeting next week. Tomorrow I'll show you how to insert the graphs. Oh, and happy first anniversary!

Easy, right? You already know how to be a good person and honor your relationships and...sorry, what did you say, dear reader? I didn't quite hear you.

"I said, what about those crazy virtues? I mean, I'm not a saint, alright? Jeez. Lay off!"

No, I won't lay off. You already know how to use the virtues as well. Stop interrupting and keep reading.

1. *Nobody ren*: Oh no! I forgot that we're meeting Japanese clients at the office today. Do I shake hands? Bow? I'd better check with someone before the meeting. I really want them to feel welcome and comfortable, and I don't want to offend.

2. *Nobody shu*: You love ice cream and keep tons of it in the house. Your friend loves peanuts and keeps a bowl on her table. Your friend is lactose intolerant. You are allergic to nuts. When you go to each other's houses, you put out fruit.

3. *Nobody li*: I hate suits. But since I'm going to my friend's wedding at the church, I should probably put one on. I know how conservative his family is.

4. *Nobody xiao*: I'm sorry. I can't go to the movie with you. I'm going to be in temple that day. I don't care about all that religion stuff, but it means a lot to my grandmother.

5. *Nobody wen*: I have an idea. Instead of the ballgame, let's head to the museum to see that rare collection of 18th Century

miniatures you love. And yes, I promise I won't make fun of it if you promise not to make thematic jokes in bed later.

The point is, you already know how to do all of this. You already do it. You already live it. Just because you aren't a Chinese citizen in 100 B.C.E. is no excuse for not cultivating the kindness, compassion, and civility already innate within you. You don't necessarily have to be a gentleman. Maybe you could just be gentle, man.

The Book of Confucius Meditation

Confucius believed in a way of heaven and harmony. Let me connect to that through restraint and self-control. May I seek to be a person of wisdom, discipline, and culture, even if I want to be the person at the party with the lampshade on my head. Stay my hand and my appetites so that at the very least, I don't forget my brother on the bus.

NOBODY'S EXERCISES

1. When your home or social life turns into a bunch of warring states, what is one (or more) way(s) you act, or can act, to restore balance?

2. When you are stressed, or living too much in one side of yin or yang, how do you get back to your center?

3. Confucius identified Five Great Relationships. Which ones do you consider the most influential in your life, and why? Who are the influential friends and mentors in your life?

4. Look again at the Confucian virtues. Which ones do you embody? Is there one you'd like to develop more in the coming months and years?

5. What does it mean to you to be a gentleman or gentlewoman? What's the smallest step you can take today to reveal your inner gentleman or gentlewoman?

6. Fill in the prompts below with one action you do or thought you have that fosters the Nobody's path to greatness in the following areas:

A. The Five Great Relationships
Nobody's ruler/subject:

Nobody's parent/child:

Nobody's older sibling/younger sibling:

Nobody's husband/wife (or any loving relationship):

Nobody's friend/friend:

B. Five Virtues
Nobody ren:

Nobody shu:

Nobody li:

Nobody xiao:

Nobody wen:

Your own meditation:

The Book of Lao Tzu

Just Go with the Flow (or Don't)

How now, eternal Tao?[1] That's a good question. Leave it to you to start out the chapter with the toughest query.

What is the Tao? The Tao is a nebulous *way*. The Tao is a principle. The Tao is like my friend's cat. I know she's somewhere in the house, but she's more a shadow and a rumor. When I look for her, she is gone. When I glimpse her, she is fleeting. I did see her once when she was cleaning herself, and she did that thing where she stretches her leg out into the stratosphere and licks it as if the lives of all inhabitants of earth depend on it. I was disgusted and envious at the same time. Does that somehow make me a bad person? It sure seems like it should.

If that example didn't help, which it probably didn't, perhaps introductory selections from the Tao Te Ching—the central 81-verse, 5000-character text of Taoism—will help us to figure it out. (Note: it probably won't, but I'll present it anyway.)

> 1. The Tao that can be trodden is not the enduring and unchanging Tao. The name that can be named is not the enduring and unchanging name. (Conceived of as) having no name, it is the Originator of heaven and earth; (conceived of as) having a name, it is the Mother of all things.[2]

4. The Tao is (like) the emptiness of a vessel; and in our employment of it we must be on our guard against all fulness. How deep and unfathomable it is, as if it were the Honoured Ancestor of all things.... How pure and still the Tao is, as if it would ever so continue! I do not know whose son it is. It might appear to have been before God.

25. There was something undefined and complete, coming into existence before Heaven and Earth. How still it was and formless, standing alone, and undergoing no change, reaching everywhere and in no danger (of being exhausted)! It may be regarded as the Mother of all things. I do not know its name, and I give it the designation of the Tao (the Way or Course). Making an effort (further) to give it a name I call it The Great. Great, it passes on (in constant flow). Passing on, it becomes remote. Having become remote, it returns.... Man takes his law from the Earth; the Earth takes its law from Heaven; Heaven takes its law from the Tao. The law of the Tao is its being what it is.

That should clear it up, no? No. You're right. It doesn't. But perhaps that is the point. Perhaps we are meant to be confused about the Tao. Perhaps we shouldn't have started our swim lesson in the deep end. Let's go back a bit and build up to this. At this point, I would advise you to return to the Confucian chapter and review our discussion of the yin and yang. I won't force you to do it, as that wouldn't be very Tao-ish of me, but you can if you feel it is right to flow that way (hint hint).

A Man and His Ox Get the Tao Outta Town

As we said, Taoism is the twin religion to Confucianism.[3] Taoism forms the serene yin to Confucianism's more active yang. But how did Taoism come to be? The short answer is: we're not sure. The longer answer begins with the idea that a man named Lao

Tzu[4] (meaning "old one" or "old child"), who may or may not have been a living, breathing man of history, blazed the path. Again, as with many of these traditions, the facts of Taoism's origin are buried under history, leaving only a scant trail back to a founder who may be more a composite of historical necessity and ideology than actual skin and bone. Nevertheless, we have the myth of this man Lao Tzu who, growing weary of his job in the archives of some Chinese state or another, hopped on a westward-moving ox toward the distant borders of China, seeking escape. Or solitude. Or a decent Mexican-food place where the salsa isn't too hot, but just hot enough. Or whatever. When he arrived at an exit point, so the story goes, a guard recognized him as a man of wisdom (likely due to Lao Tzu's long, flowing beard). The guard stopped Lao Tzu, telling him that he could not pass until he had written down his wisdom. What followed was the Tao Te Ching. It probably would have been longer than 5000 characters, but that ox wasn't going to wait forever.

Was the Tao Te Ching really the work of one great man? Or was it a compilation over centuries? Was the text originally meant to be a political tool for rooting out rival Confucian ideas? Is it simply a work of Chinese poetry? Lao Tzu's great masterpiece from a distant and lonely frontier? We may never know. But what we do know is that it is short, elegant, and so deliciously rich, it might be the religion equivalent to French cooking. Though brief, the Tao Te Ching is chock full of mind puzzles and wisdom. It is a smooth blend of give and take, centered on living in harmony with the mysterious Tao. Take a few hours to read it. Then take a life-long vacation to try to really grasp it. Good luck!

(A Not-So) Sibling Rivalry

Taoism draws power from receptive and allowing yin. But make no mistake. For all its beauty and nebulous philosophy, Taoism had a political and social point of view, and it was often in conflict with the more active Confucian doctrines. Whereas Confucianism implored a ruler to be an involved and fatherly example for his subjects, the Taoists took a more hands-off approach. Taoism encouraged rulers to allow people to live quietly in pastoral settings, free from mighty prohibitions and over-burdensome teachings. Less action, more insight. Take the following excerpts from the Tao Te Ching:

> 19. If we could renounce our sageness and discard our wisdom, it would be better for the people a hundredfold. If we could renounce our benevolence and discard our righteousness, the people would again become filial and kindly. If we could renounce our artful contrivances and discard our (scheming for) gain, there would be no thieves nor robbers.

> 20. When we renounce learning we have no troubles....

Subtle? Not exactly. I believe the message is: let's have less of those who pretend to have knowledge and more of those who are merely simple and in line with some kind of natural way. And while we're at it, less self-righteousness and crookery.

But what is the way? What is going on here? What is this Lao Tzu guy talking about? What am I talking about? I need a drink.

The Basic Tenets of Being Basic

Taoism is more than the Tao Te Ching. It is more than a man and his ox. It is an intricate lifeway. Although in its later years Taoism developed godly pantheons and religious ritual, it has its roots in philosophy. Taoism has a distinct point of view. But what is it about, exactly? What are we supposed to be viewing?

It is, as we said, all about the Tao. But what is the Tao? Why am I talking in circles and asking the same thing over and over? Good question. It's probably because I, like you, am trapped in the mind puzzles of this mysterious *way*. Trying to explain and define the Tao is like trying to explain and define the air around you. It's like trying to explain and define silence. Say I walk into a room of meditators and say, "Hey everyone, it sure is quiet in here!" Besides making an ass of myself and giving those good folks a chance to practice patience, what have I done? I have named the state of the room for sure—silence. But I have done something else, haven't I? I have destroyed the very thing I was defining. My loud, obnoxious voice simultaneously named silence and destroyed it at the same time. I'll just show myself out, thank you.

What does that example have to do with Tao? Go back a few pages and read that opening line from the Tao Te Ching. Or I suppose I could just type it again since I'm already sitting here. "The Tao that can be trodden is not the enduring and unchanging Tao. The name that can be named is not the enduring and unchanging name." Do you see the riddle? If we walk on the Tao, we're walking to nowhere and walking on nothing. If we talk about the Tao, we're really not describing it. Once we focus on the thing, we have destroyed the essence of the thing itself. It's like when Mom says, "Come and take a look at what this bird is doing!" By the time I get to the window, the bird has finished the attention-grabbing activity, or else it flies away because her voice scares it off. She actually has a nice voice. What I mean is that the sound of *a voice* scares it off. Its action was delicate. Fleeting. Once named, it disappears.

What do we do now? Well, we may be forced to define the Tao by what it is not. It doesn't really have a solid identity, though we call it something for convenience sake. I suppose we could walk up to it and call it Beauregard or something along those lines, but thankfully we don't have to. There is a pointer word—Tao—but little else. What about form? Does Tao have a form? Well, it has manifestations. We can see it manifested as a cloud in the sky or a cricket hopping merrily down a country lane, but we can't go get a handful of Tao. It's not a god or gods, and it seems to be quite disinterested in humans. In fact, in Taoism, gods would probably be as dependent on the Tao for existence as anything else. We're just here with the clouds and crickets, my friend.

In the end, maybe the best we can say is that the Tao is a *way* that is revealed in rhythms and cycles of nature. Want to experience it? Remain silent, be receptive, and go with the flow. Intuit it. Feel it. Go to the Tao Te Ching for guidance, then rely on your own natural perceptions and rhythms to bring it home. In other words, do like Yoda (I love that character, in case you hadn't noticed). He didn't have star systems at his command, right? But he was powerful, and the implication seems to be that he could have had external power if he actively sought it out. But that wasn't necessary. He didn't need accolades and palaces. He just lived in some dilapidated hut on some…oh, wait. SPOILER ALERT! He just lived in some dilapidated hut on some creature-infested planet where Luke just happens to land in just the right spot where Yoda just happens to find him. I know you're going to say, "Well, that's the power of the Force," and I understand that, it's just so unlikely that out of the whole freakin' planet, Luke just happens to… You know what? I'm sorry. Ignore that rant. I just needed to vent. I've needed to do that for decades. If you don't understand why, ask a *Star Wars* fan and they'll fill you in.

The point is, to know Tao, be still and in sync with it. Don't seek it. Don't lust after power or armies to help you find it or conquer it. The Tao is in the hut as well as the palace. It's in the murky swamp and the clear blue sky. It is with the general and the man of peace. It was here before anything, and it doesn't need anything to guide it. It just kinda...sorta...is.

Huh? What Was That?

Okay, so maybe the Tao is still nebulous, but it does form a cornerstone of a major world tradition. And someone must be enamored with the topic, because here we are talking about it so many years later. Just a note—at the time of this writing, a web search for "Tao Te Ching" brought up 425,000 results (sorry, I didn't verify every last one). Imagine that. So, much like the math textbooks I've known over the years, millions of people buy and read the Tao Te Ching, and few have a solid understanding of it. Wild.

The question we must ask is why the concept of the Tao has persisted for so long and become so popular if the concept is so elusive. Perhaps the secret lies in Taoism's focus on yin. When we work and worry in flurries of motion and commotion in the everyday life, we are quite active in body and mind. But when something comes along, no matter how confusing at first, that reminds us to be a little more flexible and receptive, it can have a profoundly calming (or confusing!) effect. Have you ever played to exhaustion in the ocean's waves, and then just floated on your back and stared up into the clouds with your ears underwater while the tide carries you along? The heart pounds in relentless rhythm, but the mind is at rest. The contrast is wonderful. In some ways, that feeling of restful flow is the core idea of philosophical Taoism, and it is reflected in a few basic concepts, such as the Tao. Let's review some of the ideas and images of Taoism and see what they say about living a better life.

Imagining the Invisible

Bear with me here as we try to anchor ourselves in some gentle discussion of Taoist concepts. Remember as you read that you must open your mind and be receptive. These aren't really concepts a person can teach. Yes, they can be defined and blogged, but to really get to the core, they must be experienced and intuited. Dad could lecture me all day on the finer points of riding a bike: pedals go around, maintain even balance on the seat, keep momentum going in my feet, eyes straight ahead. But until he let go and I could feel my energy moving the machine, with the wind in my hair and a smile plastered on my face as I wobbled down the street, it wasn't real. All the googley maps in the world can't give you the sensation of experience and place.

1. *Tao.* Uh oh. Tao again. Don't worry, I won't bang you over the head with it too much longer. Just think of it as a way or a process of nature. Remember our yin-yang picture? Well, there is a clue in there as to the nature of Tao. The forces of yin and yang are flowing and moving, giving rise to all things. They create a melody and harmony to accompany the natural rhythm of the Tao. Humanity can either sing its song without regard to rhythm—living in a scattered and wasteful way—or come into line with that rhythm and find a more natural way of voicing life. Under the latter view, we life performers don't shy away from any tune. Instead, we sing when it is time to sing and remain silent when it is time to stay silent. If we get out of tune, we don't force the notes. Instead, we wait patiently for the pitch to return to point. Hear this now: our lives produce notes of harmony and discord, but when those notes are in time and sync with the Tao, we are at peace. Let it flow. Don't get in the way.

Ah, but we do get in the way. So we need *wu-wei.*[5]

2. *Wu-wei.* If you thought Tao was a supremely awesome, mind-twisting notion, check this out. Wu-wei means "actionless action" or "natural effort." Now, what in tarnation does that mean? Actually, it's a continuation of what we've already discussed, so you're ahead! Bonus points if you know where the word "tarnation" comes from.

Essentially, wu-wei is the idea of taking only those actions and expending those efforts necessary to accomplish a task. Don't struggle! Simply allow those waves to wash you ashore. Here's another deep, spiritual explanation: sometimes I lie in front of the television and watch it with my body all crunched up on the floor. It's comfortable, so leave me alone about it. If the remote is somewhere way far away, such as on the couch above me, and I want to turn the volume up or down, I don't un-contort myself, stand up, get the remote, press the volume button, and go through all that energy-wasting effort. Sometimes I'll just extend my foot up there to the TV and hit the onboard volume button with my toe. Voila! Done! I'm not a lazy couch potato (floor potato?), but rather, someone with some flexibility who has found a way to boil an action down to its simplest form. Yes, I know the simplest form is to have the remote on the floor with me, but this is my example, alright? Sense the need and allow the answer to come spontaneously and without judgment. In other words, trust that you will know what to do.

Wu-wei asks us to consider actions, to be judicious in effort, and to do things not in a forced way, but in the natural way. The way of least resistance. Wu-wei is not instructing you to do nothing. It's not telling you to be a blob. It is asking you to listen to your intuitions, to be in tune with your body, and to be open to the flow. Separate yourself from your expectations, and trust that the path will reveal itself. Be suspicious of strictness and adherence to action for the sake of action. Politically, this may mean letting people sort some things out for themselves. In the world of finance, it's allowing the market self-correct. In education, it may suggest keeping an eye on the kids while they explore freely in the classroom so they can gravitate to their favorite subjects or activities. In art, it might be slathering paint on a canvas to see what develops. It might mean decorating with natural forms such as raw wood or natural flowers instead of exerting tons of effort into carvings, intricate arrangements, or box after box of stuff from those online design sites that claim you'll save on dining sets and rugs even when you won't.

Consider this: when I first sat down with *The Nobody Bible*—long before it was *The Nobody Bible*—it was a collection of rambling scribbles and false starts. Much like it is now. I fought with it. I tried to make it conform to my other manuscripts. I argued with the religious traditions, the humor (such as it is), and the details, trying to make it all fit some crazy ideal that can't exist anywhere but in my mind. I was paralyzed in my actual creative process because I couldn't stop wrestling with what I thought I was supposed to be doing. But one day, after finding inspiration from an unexpected source in a way I couldn't predict, I simply allowed myself to be myself and to write how I write. I realized that I had a natural voice and a natural style in my writing just like everyone else, and I simply went with it. The result (for good or for ill—you decide) is this thing you're reading right now. It wasn't forced, but just sort of came into being. The lesson? Don't schlep heavy stones to the pyramids when you can roll them on logs. Don't jump in after the fish when a perfectly good fishing pole is at your side. Don't jam the big piece of metal into the small tube in chemistry class and get your chemistry teacher all miffed because you just ruined an expensive piece of equipment and were asked to leave the room. Rather, find a better-fitting piece and let it slide right in.

Write how you write. Play how you play. Be how you feel you should be. If correction or change is necessary, then do that which is necessary. Wu-wei is your ticket to more peace and quiet. Wu-wei gets you out of the way. Wu-wei doesn't get it done, it *lets* it done.

3. *Water*. Wait. Why is water in this section? Well, in some ways, it is the quintessential essence of wu-wei and the Taoist message. How? Consider these two selections from the Tao Te Ching:

43. The softest thing in the world dashes against and overcomes the hardest; that which has no (substantial) existence enters where there is no crevice. I know hereby what advantage belongs to doing nothing (with a purpose). There are few in the world who attain to the teaching without words, and the advantage arising from non-action.

78. There is nothing in the world more soft and weak than water, and yet for attacking things that are firm and strong there is nothing that can take precedence of it;-- for there is nothing (so effectual) for which it can be changed. Every one in the world knows that the soft overcomes the hard, and the weak the strong, but no one is able to carry it out in practice.

Isn't that exquisite? The image of water does a lot of work in these two selections. Water shows us that even the softest of things can conquer the hardest. Don't believe me? Go ask the mighty solid rock walls of the Grand Canyon—the ones that still remain after water washes away their crunchy insides.[6] Water is the natural image of the power of the soft and gentle. Water is everywhere, penetrating everything, even where we can't possibly conceive. It was even on my garage roof, until I unfortunately perceived it all over the garage floor. Talk about bringing the concept of erosion home!

But the real lesson here is that water doesn't sit down and have a lengthy conversation with itself about whether to penetrate the world of rock. There isn't some guy on the rim of the Grand Canyon with a garden hose and a high-powered jet sprayer, spritzing the stones in a particular way until they fall away. Much like the elusive Tao, water simply does what it does the simple way. The natural way. The wu-wei. It follows the laws of physics as it runs downhill, gets soaked into things, and seeps into cracks when they appear in its path. Water runs a natural, humble course, and in the best of effortless effort, carves away rock over millennia despite the rock's stand of strength.

Chapter 78 (see above) of the Tao Te Ching makes this water wonder a radically powerful and practical tool, suggesting that if you want to rule a people and be their beloved monarch, you must be like water. To be truly strong, you must allow yourself to roll along in humility. You must flow with the will of the Tao, feeling what others feel. If you can take on the struggles of others' feet, you are fit to be at their head. Otherwise, what are you doing? If you refuse to take on ills or evils as they come to the people of your kingdom, then you are just an armchair ruler living in resistance. If you can't march with the infantry, don't be the general. If you remain separate from your people, you aren't in the natural flow of things as they are. You are just some distant character who is out of touch and simply throwing rules at people from a structure that looks strangely like the U.S. Capitol Building in Washington, D.C.

Be kind. Be compassionate. Be in the flow.

As you can see, water is a mighty image. It meets resistance and finds a way to continue. It carved out a large hole in Arizona with no thought of praise or reward, and then it took on the humbler role of ice in your Saturday glass of cold tea. It falls from the sky and does its wetting work, even in remote rainforests where no human has set foot. It enters and leaves our bodies, sometimes without our awareness, and in the end, it always finds a way. Is there a better metaphor for living than that?

Hold on. I'm Just a Nobody, Not Some Taoist Jedi!

[handwritten: Which one? Confucius Tao]

You're right, my friend. You aren't a Jedi. Even the Jedi weren't Jedi. They were just fictional characters that some screenwriter created to move stuff around with their minds and to live in a cool temple. We can't all be Luke Skywalker and have a master Obi-Wan to teach us the ways of receptivity, patience, and sensing the right moment to act. We don't all go with the flow all the time. In fact, we're all a bit Confucian, aren't we? We like our actions and our rules, and we enjoy telling our kids to keep their elbows off the table and to not scream and yell in public. Rules are good, right? Well, yes, I suppose they are. They help keep us safe, and they keep good order. But we also need to be flexible. We can't be all action, boundaries, and adrenaline all the time. The results that brings about are pretty awful: addiction, stress, worry, parachute jumping, selfishness...the list goes on!

Receptivity and going with the flow may sound logical, and we may want to believe that we're easygoing folks, but I encourage you to check your biases. Whenever I teach or discuss these traditions, I find that people aren't always as receptive to Taoism as, say, Confucianism. They think Taoism's philosophy of simplicity is interesting and maybe even something to strive for—and a few even have yin yang tattoos on their necks—but often, people say it's too idealistic. Too pie-in-the-sky for this busy, wired world. Many say that Confucianism feels more comfortable and structured. I'm sure even some Taoists had to "actively" seek a place where they could just go with the flow. Many of them sought refuge in the hills and lived as recluses. It's hard to escape rules, after all. Sometimes it takes effort!

Look, I get it. Many Taoist concepts seem distant, difficult, and unattainable. But I would argue that we in the regular world already live many of these elusive concepts, even though we are such active and rule-oriented folks. These principles are at work in our lives right now, helping us on our way. We know how to live in rhythm with cycles and seasons, and we have an idea of what wu-wei is really all about.

I know that when it comes to tricky concepts like this, some folks like to split hairs. They'll tie you in knots, insisting you can have a "correct" view of it all. But don't let them scare you. Gently brush these distractions out of your wu-way. No expertise is needed here. You have applied the spirit of these principles, even if they are not in lockstep with how someone else conceives of them. Be open and respectful to others when they teach or correct, but don't doubt your own interpretations. Don't be afraid to simply *know*. Just because someone tells you you're doing the puzzle wrong doesn't make their way right. And, as we just learned, sometimes dismissing the "wise" is your wisest course of action. Heck, I'm sure you've already dismissed half of what I've said in this book, and I'm not even wise! Anyway, when the moment feels right and you feel ready, read on and see how these concepts are at work in your life right now.

1. *Nobody's Tao*: Say you are a religious person, but your friend is not. Over coffee, you get into the forbidden conversation on gods and ritual. Instead of being a pointless battle of wills and arguments that will accomplish nothing, you both just kinda go with it and come to find that you do both believe in *something* bigger than yourselves. In fact, you realize that even if your friend can't name exactly what it is, it is a strong knowing within her, the same

as it is for you. It's an intuition. She doesn't have to drive anywhere to pray to it or figure it out, but she admits to you that sometimes she just sits quietly with it. You respect that about her. You go on to share your personal daily prayer with her and a few examples of how religious rituals help you connect with something bigger. The conversation is lovely all around. It flows. It gets the work done. Accord is reached on an idea with no name. Just truth and peace in spontaneous conversation.

Now, same conversation, same coffee shop. This time you are an atheist and your friend is an ardent religious devotee. You keep insisting there are no gods and no higher power. Your friend persists in her view that her chosen holy figure has it all taken care of. Eventually, you decide to sit quietly and let her say what she needs to say. Afterwards, you give her a simple hug and a smile as you always do at goodbye and make your way home listening to some good tunes. No need to say any more. No need to categorize. No need to name. It is what it is, the conversation was what it was, and the pond in your mind has no ripples.

Or imagine you are sitting alone in a forest with the wind blowing through the trees. A bird flies from the brush to the top of a nearby pine. In the distance, laughter comes from a company of hikers. These ripples of commotion don't annoy you, but only enhance the ocean of experience. The hikers, the bird, and the tree all arise from a place. This place. This moment. One thing. No name or identity required.

2. *Nobody's wu-wei*: A friend texts you a less-than-cordial message following a disagreement. You are in a huff, and your first instinct is to text back a nasty note. You need to correct the record. Right the slight. But you don't. You decide to do nothing. You stay your fingers and allow things to settle. Moments later, an apology text appears on your screen.

Maybe you are decorating your new home and are looking for the perfect table for a space behind a couch. You scour the city, but don't find anything that fits quite right. You bring some things home and try to force the issue, but it just isn't working. Eventually, you decide to hold off and leave the space alone. Then, a few weeks later, your son arrives from Texas with an unexpected piece for his home that is just the right color and size for your space. He gives it to you as a gift. Now, the space is perfect. By the way, this happened to someone I know, and it was really cool to see it unfold.

Perhaps you are in a relationship that seems to be going nowhere. One evening, you and your significant other stumble into a heated conversation about commitment. You had your heart set on watching your favorite show tonight, but such is life. At first you are ready to put up your dukes to defend yourself. However, you decide to hold your tongue and see where the conversation leads. You discover the source of the problems between you is a mutual series of miscommunications that have blocked the way. You kiss, turn on a bad romantic comedy, and move on with your lives—a little wiser about the importance of good communication and the skill of listening.

3. *Nobody's water*: You arrive from work and find your son home from school. He is struggling with an essay for English class and is ready to give up and take a failing grade. You initially yell at him to motivate him, as you usually do, and tell him he must do the assignment or you'll ground him. He quotes chapter 20 of the Tao Te Ching to you: "When we renounce learning we have no troubles." You cut him off and tell him you are feeling a little more Confucian in this conflict, and that he better get crackin' or he'll have real troubles. You storm off in a flood of angry emotions. Minutes later, undoing your tie in the mirror, you see yourself as the scared and confused young boy from your own school days,

and you remember how things were difficult and that there were times when you tried to force things until you were forced to give up. It floods upon you just how real and frightening that felt. You take your son's struggle on as your own. You decide not to resist this moment, but allow these fresh emotions to guide you in empathy. You acknowledge these feelings instead of fighting them, flow back to the kitchen, sit next to your son, and brainstorm a topic together over a soda and some cold pizza. Your son's hard façade gives way in the face of your soft demeanor, and you realize that acceptance with an embrace is often the path of least resistance.

Perhaps the woman next to you on the plane from New York wants to talk. You want to sleep. You weren't quick enough on the draw, and your iPod with the conversation-averting ear buds lays dormant in your bag. You give in to fate and reciprocate in the chat. By the time you arrive in Los Angeles, you are a little wiser on a topic of mutual interest, and you have a new business contact.

Maybe your professor tells you that you are going to fail her calculus class. In a panic, you realize this is the end of the medical school dream. You scream and argue for a place in the class, insisting that your whole future depends on it, but it's getting you nowhere. You trudge to the registrar, and in your sorrow, decide to join any ol' class. You stumble upon an offering with a new professor. He's teaching about religion in the Greco-Roman world. You are taken in by this spectacle of history and ancient learning and end up majoring in classics and religious studies. Eventually, you write *The Nobody Bible*.

Concepts in any new arena can be confusing at first, but that's only until we see how they apply. Heck, it took me until second grade to figure out how to tell time. My teacher had to take me into the hall and tutor me privately with a paper clock with two metal hands. It took many more years to appreciate the relevance of time to my life. Since then, however, I've been obsessed with punctuality and schedules—much to the annoyance of those who know me.

Taoist concepts are hard to grasp, but only until we give up the intellect-only approach and strive to understand how they fit into our daily routines. Stick with it, and I promise, if you take some additional time with these principles, it will be worth it. You're already doing it all anyway. Just go with the flow and leave the resistance behind.

Book of Lao Tzu Meditation

Allow this day to have some twists and turns. Allow this mind some confusion. Allow this body a willing and receptive spirit within. Allow a connection with all that is but that cannot be defined. Today is the day I don't fight with the mystery. Today is the day when I will intuit when to act and when to stay still. Today is the day I go with the flow. At the very least, allow me to stay in bed where I can't get into any trouble.

NOBODY'S EXERCISES

1. The Tao is a difficult concept for many folks. Do you believe in a power or a *way* that emanates all things? Does it have a name? If so, what do you call it?

2. We can't all be Taoist recluses, as we live in a world of action whether we like it or not. But what is one small way you can simplify or quiet your life in the midst of life's chaos?

3. Can you give an example of a time when you took action when maybe inaction was the better choice? How about when you didn't act when action was probably required?

4. The border guard asked Lao Tzu to write down his knowledge before he left society forever. What is a piece of knowledge you would like to leave to family, friends, and descendants?

5. Fill in the prompts below with ways that you foster the Nobody's path to allowing and receptivity in the following areas:

    Nobody's Tao:

    Nobody's wu-wei:

    Nobody's water:

    Your own meditation:

The Book of Jesus

Holy Moly! Is It Really That Simple?

The Land of Israel.[1] The Holy Land. It has, throughout its long history, been a site of great blessing, great power, and great conflict. At times open and at others oppressed, it has long been a target for takeover and a hotbed of both conflict and wonder. There is power in that ancient place. A relentless energy that permeates everything from the shawarma stands to the very bricks of the Old City. I'm sure we ascribe attributes and qualities to it that are a bit grandiose. We must not forget that it is a real city filled with diverse cultures, toy stores, coffee shops, mechanics, graffiti, shoe sellers, and all the other things one would find in any other thriving place. But then again, it has been such an impressive crossroads of religion and politics for so long that maybe it really is something more, no matter how much its citizens simply want to call it home. I guess it's like grandparents retiring near a Disney theme park. They want the grandkids to think of their summer trip as a humble journey to gramma and grampy's house, but it inevitably turns into an excuse to wait in long lines, buy stuffed mice, and eat caramel apples.

Trust me. I have relatives in Florida.

But anyway, back to Israel. The power of the Holy Land is so great, I've even heard of something called Jerusalem Syndrome.

Apparently, the sheer awesomeness of Jerusalem can overwhelm a person to the point where he or she believes they're on some kind of divine mission or are someone from the Bible. Seriously. People who seem to have it all together at the gates of Jerusalem suddenly develop religious-based psychosis on Jerusalem's soil. I don't know about that. I remember when I visited the great city, I could feel the energy and the emotion for sure, but the only divine journey I was on was to find the perfect falafel. Which I found. Twice. Would the second time be the second coming? I'm not sure, but the second one did come with fries stuffed into it and was thus heavenly in its own way.

Jesus appeared on the scene there sometime around 4 B.C.E. And yes, I know it's weird that Jesus seems to have been born before himself, but I refuse to enter that discussion too deeply here, mostly because it is too confusing to explain. Suffice it to say one of the culprits seems to be a man known as Dionysius Exiguus (470-544 C.E.), and he was apparently as bad at math as me. Or maybe he was so much better that it blew my mind and I can't comprehend it. You have the internet. Look it up if you want.

The Holy Cross(roads)

In the days of Jesus, this holy place Jerusalem was a cauldron of culture and colonization. At the time of Jesus's birth, Israel was under the control of the Roman Empire. Needless to say, many of the non-Roman people around town, including many Jewish folks, weren't thrilled with that. But what can you do when a bunch of power-hungry Romans move their chariots into town, blasting that Roman Countryman music?

Jewish groups living in the region each had their own way of dealing with the presence of the Romans. The wealthy priestly class, known as Sadducees, figured that since the Romans were there, they might as well form an alliance and get used to the change. Kind of Buddhist, right? No, probably not. They carried on with their priestly duties at the temple and moved on.

Community Jews, known as Pharisees, decided that if they had to be occupied by a foreign power, the best way to deal with it was to continue with their strict adherence to Jewish practices out in the real world. Maybe they said, "It is what it is, and I'm Jewish, so I'll just be Jewish in an occupied territory." I imagine it's a lot like today where groups of Orthodox Jews live, work, and worship in urban communities surrounded by the advance of modernity. They keep their customs, mind their heritage, and get on with the business of life as best they can. The Pharisees didn't have to be happy about the state of the world, but they could be Jewish in it. The Rabbinic Judaism you see today probably owes much to the Pharisees and their life of piety and study in the community. And, for that matter, so does Christianity, for Jesus is referred to in various places in the New Testament as a rabbi.

A third group in town, known as Zealots, were notorious for stirring up trouble in their opposition to foreign rule. Were they freedom fighters? Underminers? A group of unpleasant fellows? Who knows? It's not really for us to judge this far down the line. But one thing is for sure: they were inevitable. Colonization often comes with violent discontent, and where there is foreign rule and oppression, there is the cry for liberty and independence. Zealots will probably always have a job in this world if they're willing to relocate.

On the fringes of civilization lived a group of monastic Jews called the Essenes. The Essenes believed that the world was just too impure. They did not think much of the current priestly group running the temple back in town, thank you very much. Their solution? Move away from the hustle and bustle, abstain from pleasures, and live in poverty. They were the equivalent of modern religious studies graduate students. The Dead Sea Scrolls, discovered in a cave near Qumran by the Dead Sea (of course!), are said to be a portion of the Essene library. The Essenes believed they were living in an end of times—a time when the appearance of a messianic[2] figure would send the Romans packing and expunge the evils of the world in a great battle of light versus darkness. The Essenes practiced baptism, celibacy, and purifying rituals, preparing themselves and the world for their lord, largely based on their interpretations of holy scriptures.

Send in the Rabbi—Jesus

As they say, it's all about timing, right? And one person who had just the right timing was Jesus, arriving in this religio-political mish-mash from, as we said, roughly 4 B.C.E. until around 30 C.E. There is some speculation about where in that timeline various events occurred. But it was so long ago, we'll give historians a pass on it and just move on.

Anyway, Jesus emerged in a world hungry for change and guidance. And when such figures arrive, myth often accompanies them in their own lifetime. Remember our discussion of the Buddha and the miracles supposedly surrounding his birth? The same holds here. The Book of Matthew (1:18) records that before Joseph and Mary could consummate their marriage, Mary was found to be pregnant by the Holy Spirit. Joseph was going to quietly dissolve the marriage, but an angel appeared and told him that the child was special. The boy would be known as Jesus ("savior" or "God is salvation"), according to the Biblical prophecy in the Book of Isaiah (7:14) that a virgin would bear a child. The story only gets more familiar to us: three wise men follow the star to a lowly stable where Jesus is honored as the Son of God.

For all the "aw, shucks!" niceties of Jesus's beginnings, the tale gets muddied and difficult very quickly. Much of what we know of Jesus comes from the New Testament Gospels (Matthew, Mark, Luke, and John), set down by faithful followers starting around the year 70 C.E. We discover that this Jewish man, Jesus, was preaching with twelve faithful disciples. He healed the sick and taught for a few years before his eventual trial, crucifixion, and resurrection. There are a lot of blanks to fill in—blanks that are beyond the scope of this book. Blanks that have started wars, created schisms, and seen many people burned at the stake.

Those blanks are important and are still the topic of much debate in scholarly circles. But what we are interested in here is how what we know of Jesus today (or what is available to us) can be useful to a regular person who is still filling in the blanks of his or her own life in the modern age. Even if we don't have a crystal clear historical idea of who this Jesus was, we still have sketches and outlines. And that's good! So let's go with that.

As we said, Jesus was Jewish. He was a disrupter. He was a revolutionary. It is said that he questioned the ruling religious and political authorities and structures of his day, and for that, of course, he was not universally adored—a theme that develops around many charismatic figures. Jesus was big on love, forgiveness, and acceptance. Love. Forgive. Accept. That's gold. Jesus was about loving one's enemies, practicing forms of non-violence, and turning the other cheek:

> But I say unto you which hear, Love your enemies, do good to them which hate you, Bless them that curse you, and pray for them which despitefully use you. And unto him that smiteth thee on the one cheek offer also the other; and him that taketh away thy cloak forbid not to take thy coat also. Give to every man that asketh of thee; and of him that taketh away thy goods ask them not again.

And as ye would that men should do to you, do ye also to them likewise.[3] (Luke 6:27-31) (Emphasis added).

That last line about doing unto others is what we all know as the Golden Rule. Remember that from a few chapters back? For many folks I've talked to out there in the world of classroom and street, this little line forms the basis of their entire ethical system. Did you hear me? I said that last line forms, for many, the basis of their *entire ethical system.* One line. One statement. These are words that transcend a man and a religion and rise to the level of universal cornerstone. That is truly epic and truly Biblical. You don't have to be Christian to be a fan of this golden treasure. Many of us, Christian or not, would list this little golden nugget (or the Confucian silver equivalent) as something important to our lives whether or not we always live it.

But Jesus was more than an ethical scholar. His life and teachings are filled with other pronouncements and actions, both radical and practical. Although Jewish, he was open to new interpretations of the sabbath. Jesus was often regarded as a man of the people, known for assisting those in need. Perhaps one of the clearest pronouncements of this comes from Matthew 25:40: "And the King shall answer and say unto them, Verily I say unto you, Inasmuch as ye have done it unto one of the least of these my brethren, ye have done it unto me." Who are the "least"? The Bible verses preceding this provide a list: those who are hungry, thirsty, sick, or in prison. It also might refer to the lonely stranger on the road or the naked beggar in need of clothing. In light of these abundant plights, then, who will be deemed worthy to inherit the life beyond this earth? It's a simple answer: those who provided food, water, and comfort and those who gave companionship and the occasional shirt off their back (check out Matthew 25:34-36 for more info). Because really, in the end, if we are all children of a creator god or gods, and are part of the holy family, then what we do for one of us we do for all, and we do for this god. Seems pretty simple, right? We were all probably thinking it. It's just, Jesus (and Matthew) said it 2,000 years ago, so they get the credit. And they said it really well, so it's all good.

Two Great (and Simple) Commandments You Already Know

If we take Jesus as he is presented to us at our point in history, his whole life seems to come down to just a few things: God (in whatever sense, but for Christians with a capital "G"), and obligations to one's fellow humans. It's good to stand for things, and Jesus picked two biggies—as opposed to, say, advocating for a particular type of cola after conducting a series of Holy Land taste tests.

What else can we say about Jesus and his simple approach? Our search takes us back to the Gospel of Matthew (22:36) where we find Jesus facing a question from a Pharisee expert in religious legalities. The Pharisee asks Jesus which of God's commandments is the greatest in the law. At this point, I like to imagine a group of people debating in a town square or on some street corner, with Jesus teaching and others rabbling, peppering him with questions. No cell phones, no computers, no cameras (can you imagine?). Just the drama that no doubt unfolded around matters of religion and politics in the ancient world when much import was placed on opinion. And this question about which commandment is greatest is a rough one as, according to observant Jews, there are 613 *mitzvot* (commandments) to be found in the Hebrew Testament, comprising the backbone of Jewish practice. Imagine Jesus standing there in the wake of the question, the crowd now quiet and literally holding its breath, searching from man to man in anticipation of what this revolutionary teacher's answer might be. Which of the many rules will he choose from? And then, in one tense moment, teetering on the edge of a blade, Jesus gives the answer:

> Thou shalt love the Lord thy God with all thy heart, and with all thy soul, and with all thy mind. This is the first great commandment. And the second is like unto it, Thou shalt love thy neighbor as thyself. On these two commandments hang all the law and the prophets. (Matthew 22:37-40).

What can we take away from these simple phrases? A lot, actually. We don't have to believe that the observant Jewish folks in this tale are wrong to have 613 commandments, nor do we need to think that Jesus is being a lazy simpleton, boiling down countless years of tradition and doings into a few pithy sayings. Instead, we can consider the possibility that a master teacher is presenting his take—without judgment—on the world as he sees it. And obviously, he sees it simply:

Commandment one: Love God (or your conception of a god) with all that you have, with all that you are, and with all that you will ever be.

Commandment two: Love your neighbor as you love yourself.

It really doesn't get much simpler than that. Although, if we really get down and dirty with these two clean and neat rules, we see there is so much more afoot. What more? Why, the details of course. Jesus here presents us with an elegant solution to the problem of defining ourselves both as spiritual beings and as humans sharing a planet. Perhaps a story and conversation with him might go thus (by the way, the protagonist could be any one of us, not necessarily me):

One day in some earlyish time in the C.E.s, well after Jesus had been born before himself, a regular person like you and me was wandering through the streets at the base of the temple in the

Holy Land. He wasn't a person who favored one stance over another in this boiling cauldron of troubled times under Roman rule. He'd been to a few of the Zealot meetings, but they were too intense for him. And revolution was a huge time commitment. He certainly took pleasure in things like human contact, so the Essenes were out. No, he was just a curious guy. Down a winding path, he heard the telltale sound of a crowd in furious debate. Always up for a good argument, he decided to see what it was all about.

He dashed along the cobblestone streets, artfully dodging ox-carts and traders, almost colliding with a man selling cotton robes. "Sorry!" he yelled back as he answered the irresistible call of the crowd just ahead. He had heard stories of the great and disrupting Socrates holding court in the Greek *agora* (marketplace) 500 years before, and he knew something of that order had been stirring in this land for years under the words of another radical teacher. Could this be him?

As he approached the crowd, it was hard to get a clear view. Men swept up in a whirlwind of anger and frustration were directing questions and insults at an as-yet unseen figure pushed up somewhere in a doorway. The common man of no particular station forced his way into the mob, pushing and squeezing until he caught sight of the rabbi Jesus—calm and collected—taking it all in stride, one question and one answer at a time.

"Jesus!" screamed the common man, "I'm not sure what I stand for. I feel that I have a purpose here, but I can't quite figure it out. Can you help me?"

Their eyes met with smiles and the rabbi held up his hand. In a near whisper, he asked the crowd to silence. Out of some unseen respect, a hush fell onto the street and the people waited in anticipation for something to happen. Then, the teacher spoke.

"Young man, thank you for your question. You want to know your purpose?"

"I do." The man's voice trembled in earnest anticipation. "I want to know what it's all about."

"It's simple," came a voice to his right. A Pharisee stepped forward to make his case. "Follow the laws, for it is in laws where man finds the discipline that yokes him to God. And notice I'm using a capital 'G,' so you know it's important!"

"I do follow the laws," the common man said. "As best I can. And heartfully."

Jesus's smile deepened before he interjected. "So wherein lies your problem?"

"The problem is that I feel there is something missing. Or that there is something deeper and simpler that underlies all these rules and regulations."

The crowd raised their din behind the query, and the commoner could feel the push of the masses—now angered that one so green and uninformed would dare to question the law. The scholar to his right yelled out, "He wants simplicity! This man of no repute wants simplicity! Let us then ask the great rabbi. What is the simplest of the laws for this young man to follow? Go on, rabbi! Make it simple!"

A hush again fell as Jesus closed his eyes, taking in a deep breath. When he opened them again, a smile as broad as the Holy Land itself shone on his face. "Young man, do two things. Love your God with all your heart and soul, and love your neighbor as you love yourself. Then you will have the simplicity you seek."

An angry tide was again rising in the stunned crowd. With renewed vigor, the common man stepped in and addressed those assembled.

"Listen to me," he said. No one heard. But then, this nobody in particular found his voice and his courage, and he bellowed with confidence, "Listen! The rabbi's response is a victory for all of us. If we heed the mitzvot with a full heart, then we truly love God with all that we are. That is the first truth. And if we love our neighbor as we love our own selves, then surely we honor God and creation beyond any measure here known. That is the second truth. These two commandments are important not because they replace tradition or the laws, but because they put them in context—God and humanity stand together as one, each a reflection of the other."

And with that, nods and sounds of approval rolled through those assembled on that street below the temple. It was suddenly understood that all stood for one thing. In the light of this new understanding, the vociferous and hardened mob melted back into the streets in quiet pairs and groups eager to further discuss and understand before the sun set into the sabbath. The scholar, who only moments before tormented the common man, came to take his arm—leading him away for a meal at his home. The nobody in particular turned back to thank the great teacher, but he had vanished into the twilight.

⁕ ⁕ ⁕ ⁕ ⁕

Did it happen this way? Is this how Jesus made his great two-pronged announcement? Probably not. But this scene of a mob—newly enlightened under a peaceful accord—dispersing into an evening of good-natured chitchat is how I like to envision it. I like to think of a world where sides once opposed come together in reason and good feeling in the embrace of open-minded debate. Maybe that makes me a naïve Pollyanna, but so what? Someone has to be. Hey, where would this world be without that annoyingly cheerful neighbor whose constant good humor cancels out the energy of at least 10 crotchety curmudgeons on the block? Anyway, my little story above conveys the idea that flexibility and simplicity need not signal the destruction of tradition. No matter how convinced you are that this or that action is divine decree or ordained by a god, civility and tolerance in an organized society demand you accept that your neighbor's traditions may differ. You don't have to agree, you certainly don't have to join, and no one says you should decorate your house in the same colored lights each December. However, decency dictates that you dialogue and find a common ground.

Two for the Road

We're all walking this path to our own conceptions of self-improvement. But alas, we're so busy! It's so gosh darn hard to improve when we can't get a moment's peace. There's not a lot of room in our day for tons and tons of religious facts and figures or spiritual seekingness. We're sunk, right? Nope. You now know that we have these amazingly refreshing Two Great Commandments from Jesus. Could this really be all we need to find a little more peace? Could it really be that these profound teachings are hiding in plain sight all around us, ready to improve our lives? Here are some examples of how you already live them.

1. *How Nobody loves God (or any conception of higher power)*: A surgeon has a patient who has asked him to pray with her family in the hospital chapel. While he respects her Catholic beliefs, he follows a different religious path where praying with others of a different faith is discouraged. He's not sure he can be part of her prayer circle. But then again, he feels like his life in healing is a call from god, and he seeks to bring god glory. Maybe if he quietly holds space with his patient and her loved ones while they pray in heartfelt devotion to a supreme power, it will bring glory to his conception of god and to this surgeon's noble profession.

Or maybe a woman discovers that one of her coworkers is violating company policy and the law. He is padding sales numbers to increase his year-end bonus. The woman is not religious, but she does have a strong sense of ethics and she wants to do what's right. She lets her manager know what's going on so that he can take the proper steps to ensure the issue is investigated and dealt with properly. A person doesn't have to have god in her life to have ethics. Sometimes doing the right thing is the highest conception of power.

Not part of an organized religion, but still feel a spiritual closeness with a power of some sort? That's fine. You still live out—or could easily live out—the first great commandment. Create a daily ritual that connects you to that power. Say a prayer of gratitude at sunrise or sit in meditation for a few minutes and focus on the gift of breath filling your lungs. Or be still for a moment and remain mindful of the blessings in your life that flow from a pure, clean connection to whatever brings you great meaning and joy.

2. *How Nobody loves my neighbor as myself:* What if I am agnostic on the issue of a god? In other words, I can't say for sure if such a power exists one way or the other. Maybe in that case, I feel like my community of friends and neighbors is something like a higher power. I can still contribute. I can still show love. I can keep someone in need in my thoughts and put some good energy out there for him. Maybe I can work a few hours a week for the benefit of my community, realizing that I am just one of many energies that make up the colorful fabric of my society.

Perhaps I am a Jewish parent and my kids want to sing in a community choir. The problem is that they will sing Christmas music, and my family doesn't do Christmas. But you know? Some of that music is powerful and touching. Perhaps this is a time for

me to put the tolerance and humanity of my tradition into practice. If my children come from a strong Jewish background in my
home, maybe it's possible to share the beauty and artistic bounty
of a neighbor religion. Maybe I can even have some of my kids'
non-Jewish choir friends over for a latke party, teach them *dreidel*
(a spinning top used on Hanukkah) games, and tell the story of the
temple oil that lasted for eight days. After all, miracles aren't only
for Jewish folks. Education of others is mandatory if we want to
reduce stigma, ignorance, and indifference in our communities.
When neighbors participate in one another's traditions and come
together in song and celebration, it does much to improve community morale and understanding.

Or this: I live in an apartment complex with thin walls. I know
that my music can probably be heard through the walls. Maybe I'll
get a good set of earphones for the evenings when I know everyone else is home from work and wants to relax, too.

This isn't magic, folks. You don't have to be a monk, rabbi, or
priest to do this. You don't have to have graduated from a semi-
nary, studied religion, or have been raised by a particularly pious
pack of wolves to know that what is simple is often the most effective. Just because Jesus is a religious figure doesn't mean his
wisdom won't apply in non-religious or non-Christian contexts.
After all, common sense suggests that putting loving attention on
neighbors and our community would go a long way to making us
all a lot happier, no matter our background.

Book of Jesus Meditation

May I find the strength to occasionally go against the herd, even if it makes me unpopular. May I know in my heart that there is simplicity behind the complex and that an honest search can often reveal great truth hiding right here in my world. When my life gets to the point where I want to rip out my hair and the hair of the tall person in front of me at the movies, clop me on the noggin and remind me: love the universe and love the person in front of me, even if he is driving me crazy. For someday, I may be the one driving everyone else crazy.

NOBODY'S EXERCISES

1. Is there a principle in your life for which you would sacrifice your life?

2. Okay, so you didn't die for the thing(s) you love in question one because you made it to question two. What are some principles for which you have stood up, and how have you stood up for the principles and people you love?

3. How important are rules to you? What rules do you follow in your life, and how do they help you to stay focused and disciplined? What do you do when you disagree with a rule?

4. Do you agree with the Two Great Commandments? If yes, why? If no, why not? What would your two cornerstone rules for living be?

5. Humor me and assume you do agree on some level with both commandments. Fill in the prompts below with ways you live them in your life (keeping in mind that "god" is a relative term in this book).

I show love for (my own conception of) a god or gods or the universe by:

I show love for my neighbor by:

Your own meditation:

The Book of Brahman

Is There a Way off This Wheel?

Have you ever had a conversation with a little child? I'm not talking about the fun conversations concerning video games and candy. I'm talking about the intense, gut-wrenching, existential conversations that reveal just how much we take for granted as the boneheaded adults we are. Perhaps this isn't even your child. Perhaps you are trapped because you are at a friend's house, and you can't be rude to someone else's kid, right? I mean, you can't tell someone else's kid to buzz off. Maybe it goes like this:

"Ow!" I reached down to massage my shin. "Billy, why did you kick me?"

"Are you my daddy's friend?" Billy stared up at me with a dirty, crooked sucker stick dangling precariously from his mouth. It probably had something sweet attached to it days ago. Months ago. But no longer. Then again, maybe he found it in the driveway after someone else had enjoyed the good part.

"Yes, I'm your daddy's friend," I replied, trying my best to put out a patient, surrogate vibe that bore a sharp edge akin to a butter knife…or scissors from a kindergarten art class. "I'm here to watch the game and eat nachos like I do every Sunday. Even before you were born! It's my day of rest. Do you rest? Do you like to take naps? How about a nap?"

"What's your name?"

"You know my name. I just saw you last week."

"Where do you come from?"

"America."

"Where did America come from?" Billy wasn't giving up.

"Um...well..." Did he mean this literally or philosophically? Can kids his age think philosophically? I decided to punt and give my very best answer. "I donno."

"Are you from earth?"

"No." Ha! Confusion. That was a good tactic to derail him.

"Where did earth come from?"

"Uh...er...space?"

"Where did space come from?"

"That's...well, that's...Don!" I yelled back to the kitchen. "Don, how are those nachos comin'? You need any help in there? The game's at commercial." Silence. Don was no dummy. He was taking a break of his own. Billy, however, took no breaks.

"Where did the sky come from?"

"Everything came from the big bang, okay? You'll get to that in high school, along with acne, puberty, and teasing." Nice. Scare the kid. "Now, go see what your mommy is doing in her room."

"Mommy says I can't bother her when she's in there with the door closed."

"Oh. That's too ba—"

"Where did high school come from?"

In a hushed whisper, I finally decided to level with him.

"High school comes from the Devil, kid. You know about him, right? Legend says he comes for the souls of little children who ask too many questions."

Billy's eyes grew as wide as saucers. I could tell he was working through the theological details to decide if this was something he should be concerned about.

"Where did the Devil come from?"

"God," I said casually, resigned to testing out my religious theories on a blank slate.

"Where did God come from?"

"Hmm…" Checkmate. Well-played, little one. I decided to concede defeat, as the commercials were ending. "Billy," I said, ready to give my ego a rest, "you have bested me in our little chicken-and-the-egg game. I bow to you and your ceaseless line of questioning, more damaging to me than bullets. Now go and be at peace with your action figures and your soggy graham crackers and your bacteria sucker and let me watch football."

(Uneasy pause…)

"Where did football come from?"

* * * * *

Got it? Sound familiar? Good. Now you're ready to discuss Hinduism. You see, that (unfortunately not so) fictional conversation with a young child is something on the order of what I get when Hinduism shows up in class. When we have questions about the world's religious traditions, we can usually find something to satisfy our curiosity. Sure the explanations often bring on more questions, but that's okay. The answers may be based on sacred story and faith, mystical journey and fancy. Maybe even a hint of agenda. You know many of these answers already: Buddha, Moses, Jesus, the Bible, Muhammad, Abraham, the Apostles' Creed, Lao Tzu, the Tao Te Ching, birth from a virgin, or a place on the map in some faraway land. In other words, we have central doctrines, founders, clear denominations, and unifying statements. Even though the facts surrounding religion are often hazy, we can make our way through and satisfy our need to know. We can trace a history or pin something down. But with Hinduism? Well, with Hinduism, it's not always so clear.

Let me just give you some disclosure right up front: if you are an armchair religious historian looking for a central founder for Hinduism, forget it. That's right. Toss it out. There is no one in the office. The store is closed. The curtains are drawn. The phone will just keep ringing off the hook. Billy will talk to an empty armchair with that gross sucker stick hangin' from his lips. There is no single person who stepped forward to take on the mantle of Hinduism's flesh and blood founder. In fact, many Hindus believe this path has wended forever, without beginning. Neat.

Next you're going to ask if there's a rock-solid core belief that all Hindus must hold to be part of the tradition, like a specific creed or a mandated way of thinking about god. Surely there must be one central, orthodox (I'm going to use a technical term here) *thing*, right? Well, it's more of a collection of themes. One *particular* god or gods? Um…that's complicated. Central figure? We already said no, Billy. One big temple that everyone should go to as part of a grand act of faith? *Ehhh!* (That's the sound of a buzzer from one of those '80s game shows.) Even "Hinduism" and "Hindu" give us trouble because they are terms that came largely from outside the tradition itself.[1] Hinduism is an ancient and rich history. It is a complex blending. It is a connection of historical traditions across cultures that met and mixed.

When you are looking at Hinduism, don't use one lens. Imagine that you are using a microscope with the different magnifications—the one you played with in high school until you broke it. When seen from far away, there are some broad, common themes in Hinduism—ideas that repeat or sacred stories that are popular. But as you get closer and closer, you see there is a profound diversity and specialization that in some ways defies explanation and classification. It is a series of unique, yet related, strains that create a complex and wonderful system. Have you ever eaten a pomegranate? From the outside it is a unified, red bundle that you call "pomegranate." But cut it open and what happens? Cells of juicy fruit tumble out. Yes, these little pods come from the same bulb, but each has its own shape. Its own level of sweet and juicy. You have one giant piece of fruit composed of unique, sweet parts. Pomegranate, yes. Uniform, no.

I Don't Like Pomegranates. Now What?

Relax. Think of it this way: just because we can't explain what came before the big bang (if that's how this all came to be) doesn't mean we don't have forests, streams, fish, and red velvet cake, right? Worry less about *why* and get more into *why not*. You are here and breathing, even though the thing that came before everything is unknown and unnamed. If it becomes known after this book goes to print, feel free to cross out this paragraph. Take Billy as an example (oh no!), but then take it a step further. When questions such as "Where did the gods come from?" and "Where did the big bang come from?" trouble you more than they trouble a salaried academic, go out and take a walk in the natural world that is here nonetheless.

Wait. Where was I before I went off on that tangent with no apparent beginning? That's right—Hinduism. Let's get back to that. There are, as we said, elements of Hinduism that we can examine and study, even if the tradition doesn't fit neatly into our preconceived notions and boxes. We can find some things to latch onto even if we don't know all the answers. And maybe that's good for you. Maybe you are too set in your ways and need a little shakeup from your comfortable notions of the religious. I certainly do.

I know, I know. Some of you are still upset that it isn't all neat and tidy with starts and finishes, yeas and nays, and chocolate or vanilla. In that case, let's have a little history to clean the palate and settle the stomach. But remember, the jury is still deliberating over many of these facts and figures. Take it upon yourself to do some additional research. What's your point of view?

A Little History, a Giant, and Plumbing

The roots of the families of religious tradition in India that we commonly refer to as "Hinduism" might be traced to a place called the Indus River Valley in modern Pakistan and northwest India. Archaeologists have discovered evidence of a group that lived in this area around 3,000 B.C.E. called the Harappa culture. There is evidence of a writing system and complex cities built to defined plans. Intricate homes, some apparently with bathrooms and plumbing, have also been discovered. Archaeologists have also found currency with seals (not the oceanic kind) imprinted on it. One such seal shows a naked man with a headdress seated in meditation. Some believe this is an early depiction of the god Shiva, whom many Hindus revere today. Places of worship, as well as idols, have been identified. That tips us off to a vibrant religious life. Pretty amazing. I probably would have enjoyed living there. I don't really need cell phone towers or a television. Any place with a bathroom and running water is fine by me.

What happened next? Well, no one is really sure. Some say the Harappa culture declined due to drought or political issues (do times ever change?). Was it an invasion? Migration? A slow mixing-in through immigration and intermarriage? Who knows? Where there is a great community there is often great competition, and some scholars believe that around 2000 to 1500 B.C.E., folks from northwest and central Asia started to trickle in to this valley. They were known as Aryans, or nobles. They had horses, sheep, and a warring mentality. They also had a defined class structure. In other words, they divided folks up into categories to determine social class. It's what we could call a caste system: priests, warriors, and regular folks like you and me (see how ancient we are?!?). When the Aryans conquered a group, guess where the conquered folks went? That's right! They went into a fourth group known as servants, under the foot of the lowest class.

The Aryans had a full-on religious system consisting mostly of nature deities. There was a great father god known as Dyaus Pita ("Sky Father"). There was also Agni, the fire god; Indra, the storm god; as well as gods of wind and justice. The student favorite, Soma, was the god of altered states. He had his own drink and everything. That was probably a good drink. I think it bestowed immortality. Modern energy drinks only make you *think* you're immortal.

Fire and religious offerings were a hallmark of this Aryan religion, and the priests ruled the show. There were animal and food sacrifices as well as sacred hymns that traveled through time from priest to priest. The collection of hymns forms the *Rig Veda* (probably composed around 1500 B.C.E.), the earliest and one of the most revered Hindu scriptures. By the way, many Hindus believe Vedic literature, like the religion, has no beginning. It always was, and is. Three other texts make up the core of the Vedas, with instruction on ceremonies, prayers, and sacrifice.

It is in *Rig Veda* 10:90 where we find something like a creation story. It is the tale of the world forming from a man before time—Purusha. He was a giant of sorts, and the subject of a Vedic sacrifice. From this one man came the many manifestations of life today. Remember that image for later. Also, this story is used to justify the four castes and the primacy of priests who, after all, supposedly keep the world spinning with their priestly duties. How did the gods divide up Purusha? Well, they made his mouth into priests and warriors from his arms. Merchants came from his thighs, and servants came from his feet. The moon, sun, sky, and some of the gods came from him, too.

In this one story, gods, priests, the social system, and the things of the universe have their divine origins explained. Set for time. If you are a servant, you are a servant because of this divine origin. If you are a priest, you are a priest because of this divine origin. If you were in the lowest of groups, I suppose you could argue with Purusha about it, but it probably wouldn't do much good. This is the power of sacred story and sacred myth. It not only provides guidance, but structure. In the case of Purusha, that structure has not only spiritual and religious ramifications, but social and political ramifications as well.

Thanks for the History, but I'm Still Lost

I delved into that history not because I wanted to indulge my history-writing skills (such as they are), but because I believe it's important to know that the family of Hindu traditions we see today comes from an older history. Disputed, yes, but older. It is built upon something. Also, the historical narrative is an anchor that can ground our further study. Like I said, the history is far more complex and controversial than I have presented here, but it serves as a jumping-off point for thinking about the underpinnings of Hindu tradition.

Good? Good. I want you to note that the Vedas end with a series of later writings known as the Upanishads, which have their origins around 500 B.C.E. (although some may have been written earlier). This was a critical period in history, because many great thinkers including Buddha, Socrates (we'll meet him later), Confucius, and Lao Tzu were stirring the philosophical pot at about this juncture. The Upanishads take us beyond the priestly fires and sacrifices of the older portions of the Vedas and are somewhat more philosophical in tone. Many of their concepts form the themes of Hindu tradition and probably include some things you've read about in the New Age section of your local bookstore. Oh, and in case you're wondering, most of that stuff in the New Age section isn't new.

The Upanishads are conversations intended to extend and clarify. In fact, the word Upanishad means, in essence, "sitting down near," evoking the image of students learning at the feet of their masters. Imagine groups of unsatisfied seekers (remember the Buddha?). Perhaps they see the priests doing their Vedic thing in the village square, but say to one another, "Why can't we regular folks have access to some of this stuff? I mean, isn't there a bit more to life than just watching other people do fire and sacrifice? I may be nobody in particular, but I still have things I want to study and accomplish." So they wandered into the woods or went down by the river and found teachers who could take them into higher realms of insight. They wanted to meditate. They wanted to find spiritual unity with whatever is out there. They wanted a personal practice. This, perhaps, is the origin of many of the insights in the Upanishads.

One, Many, Karma, and More!

Now that we are somewhat better oriented to history, books, names, and whatnot, let's take a closer look at Hindu tradition. Read carefully, test your own worldview against these concepts, and see where you stand. If you feel unbalanced, please feel free to stand down.

1. *Atman and Brahman*. Let's start at the potential beginning with Brahman. It is said that Hindu culture has many gods, including Shiva (the destroyer), Brahma (the creator), and Vishnu (the preserver). Other gods and goddesses, such as Lakshmi, Saraswati,

and Ganesha, are also quite popular. Many Hindus show their devotion to one of these particular gods, but possibly more. For example, they may make offerings at a temple of Shiva or give respect to the elephant god Ganesha before they pray to one of the other gods. But the question is, are these really many gods or simply manifestations of something more supreme? That is up for debate, but there are clues. The Upanishads discuss the concept of Brahman (not the god "Brahma"—it's spelled differently). Brahman is an ultimate, supreme reality that is at the core of all appearances, that manifests all things, and that is all in one. For example, check out this excerpt from the Kena Upanishad (3:I):

> Brahman is the vast ocean of being, on which rise numberless ripples and waves of manifestation. From the smallest atomic form to a Deva [god] or an angel, all spring from that limitless ocean of Brahman, the inexhaustible Source of life. No manifested form of life can be independent of its source, just as no wave, however mighty, can be independent of the ocean....[2]

If we take this passage to its far reaches, we (or maybe just me—you may see something different) see that really, in the end, all things are manifestations of Brahman, or the supreme reality. All is, in essence, one thing. Criminal and victim, sea and sky, wood and flame. Anything that may seem opposed, or even independent, is a manifestation of one reality. Once we get through our ignorance and realize that all things (even the gods?) are just ripples in the vast ocean of Brahman, the dream of life vanishes into truth. Let me just say here that I am talking about one point of view in Hindu philosophy called Advaita Vedanta, best espoused by the philosopher Shankara around 800 C.E. But not everyone sees it that way. Other schools of thought differ in their conception of what "ultimate" is all about, but those go way beyond the scope of this book. If you're looking for a little more discussion on this topic, search for the terms Advaita Vedanta and Dvaita Vedanta on the internet. Let me know what you come up with.

Anyway, remember our discussion of yin and yang? I hope you were paying attention! This point of view is similar. Look back at that figure of the yin and yang. Imagine that you could spin it on the page really, really fast. Black and white would merge into a spinning blur, each side indistinguishable from the other. What you thought were solid black and white sides become joined in an ocean of gray, with all distinguishing characteristics gone. Your whole perception of the world changes in an instant. No thing can exist in this world without its opposite because all things and their opposite are one.

Is there anything about us that is unique, or is it all a manifestation from one thing? Good questions. I'm glad you asked. The short answer is that it's confusing and I'm not sure. As for a longer answer? Well, some say we have a piece of that supreme ultimate, Brahman, within us. In other words, we contain something called Atman. Atman is the animating gift from Brahman. It is the essence of our *self* beyond what we think we are—beyond preferences and particularities. It is the "s"elf to the "S"elf. It is the part of Brahman in me that watches as I play in the sandbox of temptation. It is there with me as I wander the world of senses and limitations. It is waiting for me to realize its existence and to realize I am part of something bigger. If I go deep enough into my deepest self, I discover that at my core I am actually Brahman (ripples in oceans, anyone?). My personal Atman is Brahman. My little self is identical to the big Self. I am, then, a really big "S"! Wait, that doesn't sound right. I'll just say that I am the ultimate source! Think of Atman as the silver cord tethering you to your Brahman foundation. Within the confines of a materialistic world I come to believe, quite naturally, that I am separate from the sacred and floating free in chaos. However, if I have the right mind and discipline, I can reel myself back in to the ultimate truth: *I am the thing that tethers me.* In the end, the categories of my personal self and the ultimate reality dissolve into one. Confused? Good. Me too. We can start a club, charge dues, and wear matching shirts.

Here is an excerpt from the Chandogya Upanishad to clarify what we just discussed: "All this is Brahman. Let a man meditate on that (visible world) as beginning, ending, and breathing in it (the Brahman)."[3] (III.14.1)

You see? All this time you felt alienated from source, when really, the source was in you all along. Just remember, it's not so easy to get in touch with it even though it lives in the house with us. Why? Because we live in a state of *maya*—illusion or unreality. Instead of seeing the reality of the Atman-Brahman thing and letting go of our illusions, preferences, and such, we keep ourselves locked in this material world of appearances. We believe we are separate and different from ultimate reality, striving for goals we think are taking us down the superhighway. But they're merely tangential side-trips. We let our true being attach to things that have no lasting truth instead of linking to the true and lasting Brahman. Why? How? Panic! (Don't panic. We're all in the same boat, and billions of panicking people will just be too dangerous.)

2. *Samsara and moksha.* Here we are, all of us this one supreme thing. And here we are all trying to merge with that thing (knowingly or unknowingly). So what's the problem? The problem is that we are trapped in samsara, or the wheel of life. We go through rebirth after rebirth—body after body—in reincarnation trying to attain moksha, or liberation from the wheel. We come back again and again trying to get it right. We go around and around until we discover the ultimate truth. The Upanishads regard the moksha escape as the greatest of goals. Oh, and remember Buddha? Remember suffering? Well, this should sound very familiar.

3. *Karma*. Why do we live so many lifetimes? Why do we have to spin on the wheel of samsara? I can't even watch Wheel of Fortune without getting a little woozy. I don't want to spin around and around, lifetime after lifetime, until I throw up. It's like the time my friend Dave convinced me to go on a carnival ride called the Zipper. Not only did it revolve on a swinging arm, but the individual carriages on the swinging arm went around and around. My "friend" flipped us over and over as this thing spun and it was all quite terrible. I asked (read: yelled at) him to stop, like, a million times, but Dave has selective hearing. I'm getting dizzy just writing about it. When we got off, I collapsed on the curb and he had a hot dog. That, my friends, is a study in suffering.

But why so many rebirths? Why do we have to be reborn as cockroaches, plants, animals, and friends of Dave? Why can't we achieve liberation? The answer lies, in part, in karma—that impartial (although some say it is divinely allotted) law of cause and effect that states that our actions and thoughts have consequences for which we must answer. For example, Dave must come back as someone upon whom I will vomit after getting off a future Zipper. Or he must be a hot dog.

Karma is so familiar to us. We lament it. We fear it. It has crept into our modern lives to such an extent, we use it in casual speech. For example, if someone is acting in a way we find distasteful, but then they suffer for it, we say, "Ha! Karma sucker!!!" Let's face it. We want to believe in rewards to come. We want to bask in the sunshine of life. We want our cold and isolated lives to be absorbed in the shining light and unifying fire of Brahman. We want to be *enlight*ened. However, we suffer (or succeed) in this lifetime because of past deeds. We come back to answer for those deeds until we can finally achieve release from samsara. Moksha!

According to the Chandogya Upanishad:

Those whose conduct has been good, will quickly attain some good birth, the birth of a Brâhmana [priest], or a Kshatriya [warrior], or a Vaisya [merchant]. But those whose conduct has been evil, will quickly attain an evil birth, the birth of a dog, or a hog, or a Kandâla [outcaste].[4] (V.10.7).

How do we get off the spinning wheel? We must know when enough of life is enough. In other words, enough with the notion that we are not connected to the ultimate (whatever it is). Enough with the idea that things should be other than they are. Simply find the nest of Brahman and rest in peace. When that happens, you will have what you truly seek. You will have release. Barring that, you can sit next to me on the curb while Dave has another hot dog.

Get Me off This Crazy Wheel Any Way You Can!

That stuff about escaping the wheel sounds good. We'd all love to be rid of our cravings and potentially harmful desires. We want to find release, but we just don't know how. How the heck do we get off the karmic Zipper to grab that divine hot dog? What's the secret? That is the million-dollar question. I guess you could think of life like the Department of Motor Vehicles—millions of people crammed into the place, tons of lines, zillions of forms, and a constant quest to figure out the system. There are some tips and tricks, and you do your best, but in the end, it takes patience. Sooner or later you'll get your license. Such are the Hindu paths to moksha. Various Hindu texts suggest that through self-discipline, one can come to know Brahman. In other words, a person can transcend the limited view of the self and gain the highest perspective. And eventually, escape.

Great. But where do we start?

Some folks seek liberation through devotion to a particular deity, and some folks head for the mountains to meditate. The

Bhagavad Gita, another revered Hindu text, tries to provide some answers. The Gita is a conversation between Prince Arjuna and Lord Krishna, a manifestation of the Hindu god Vishnu. Arjuna is in battle against his cousins and elders and he doesn't want to fight them. What's a guy to do? Well, he decides to do nothing but sit and wait. But Krishna, disguised as Arjuna's chariot driver, tells Arjuna he should do his duty as a member of the warrior class (remember our Aryan friends and their multi-tiered society?). In other words, all people must do their assigned duty in this life, even killing on the battlefield. In essence, the recipe is to be reborn to a body to work out your karma, do your duty in service to the divine, and realize that you will return again. In the end, you will discover that what is truly lasting in a person is greater than this temporal existence. Think of it this way: if you take a rebirth as a great warrior, and in your lifetime a just war comes upon you and your people, then your duty is to fight. If you're worried about killing others, just remember that what is divine and lasting in them cannot truly be killed.

In the Gita, Krishna reveals paths one might take to bring his or her awareness to the divine and the divine will. These are called *yogas*. These yogas aren't just the thing you do in between text messages on Thursday nights at the gym, although that might be part of it. The yogas are methods of yoking oneself to the divine. In fact, "yoga" comes from a Sanskrit word meaning "to unite" or "to join." How do we go about yoking ourselves to, and joining, divinity?

1. *Bhakti yoga*. This practice is devotion to an incarnation of the divine, and it is a biggie. In fact, in chapter nine of the Gita, Krishna tells Arjuna:

Which of the yogas seems right for you?

> If one of evil life turn in his thought Straightly to Me, count him amidst the good; He hath the high way chosen; he shall grow Righteous ere long; he shall attain that peace Which changes not...Be certain none can perish, trusting Me![5]

Just in case that doesn't convince you how powerful devotion can be, consider this from the Gita, chapter 18:

> Listen! I tell thee for thy comfort this. Give Me thy heart! adore Me! serve Me! cling In faith and love and reverence to Me! So shalt thou come to Me! I promise true, For thou art sweet to Me! ... And let go those—Rites and writ duties! Fly to Me alone! Make Me thy single refuge! I will free Thy soul from all its sins! Be of good cheer!

In other words, devote yourself to a manifestation of god, give offering and glory, and there will be release. Think about the words followers use about Jesus. Do Krishna's words sound familiar? If so, then you're penetrating to the heart and power of bhakti across traditions.

2. *Karma yoga*. This is different than the karmic law of cause and effect we discussed earlier, yet related. "Karma" comes from the Sanskrit word for "action." In karma yoga, one adopts the practice of selflessness and selfless doing. Like Arjuna, you must do your duty without thought of reward or potential ills. Simply do what you must. If your mind is always trained on the rewards you will get from your actions, you'll be bound to the cycle of suffering (my goodness, that word!).

If, for example, an artist paints simply to see his works in fine art galleries, then he will be disappointed and depressed if those works never make it there. The key is to simply create because it is what you are here to do. Paint to paint. Making art for the sake of creating it is the highest principle. Everything else is of lesser concern.

If you take an action, and then become seduced by the rewards or lack thereof, you accrue more—say it with me—karma! Oh, and suffering. Yes. Suffering, too. Those of you who yelled that out are also correct. Anyway, when you get attached, annoyed, impatient, or yell, instead of just doing what you need to do in a selfless way, you accrue more karma and you may have to return to deal with it. According to this path of karma yoga, you are striving for zero. You want to get and owe nothing. Receive your rebirth, do your selfless duty, and eventually the urges with which you were born will melt away. You can link your will with the divine will in a chain of action that just might pull you to release.

3. *Jnana yoga*. This is the pathway of knowledge. It's about discovering the truth of Brahman as the one source via disciplined investigation in the pathways of the mind. Perhaps you start with basic learning. Study the Gita. Study the Upanishads. Watch the parts of *Star Wars* where Yoda is talking. Dialogue with teachers and gurus who are blazing the trail ahead of you. But then? Well, then delve into your thoughts. Get to know who you truly are. Figure out that whole Atman-Brahman thing and seek to understand it. Meditate deeply on it. Then, meditate some more. Breathe. Consider. You can come to understand the nature of the unity of things through study and contemplation. In other words, you escape the binding wheel by overcoming your misconceptions about life. In time, you will come to perceive the real unity that exists behind apparent dualities.

4. *Raja yoga*. Raja yoga is also known as royal yoga. It was first set down by the sage Patanjali some time between the first century B.C.E. and the second or third century C.E. (although, no one knows for sure). Raja yoga is a map to better living through eight steps, or limbs. It was Patanjali's belief that through this practice, one could connect with his or her true spirit and find union with

the supreme. The eight stages cover ethical living, mental disciplines, physical control, and meditative practice. A full treatment is beyond this book, but here are the steps in broad strokes: in the first stage, one adopts a mindset of non-harm to living things. One must also control greed and lust, and speak honestly. In the second stage, one maintains cleanliness as well as restraint in speech and thought. Stages three, four, and five are about proper physical posture, breathing, and sense detachment. In stages six, seven, and eight, a person devotes oneself to concentration, meditation, and bliss states. That final stage of bliss is the union of person and divinity.

You should hear echoes here of the Buddha's Noble Eightfold Path—again, assuming you didn't start with this chapter. If you did start with this chapter, go back and read the Buddhism chapter and then come back to this page and you should hear echoes here of the Buddha's Noble Eightfold Path. We'll wait for you.

Ultimate release, then, is more than stretching and more than sitting quietly. It is an inextricably intertwined way of being, disciplining, and experiencing. In other words, one finds ultimate release in self-mastery—mastery of body, mind, and soul.

It's a Lot, but You're Starting to Get off the Wheel

We've come a long way in this chapter. We've discovered that our personal Atman and the great Brahman could very well be one and the same. We've learned that it is our desires and expectations that keep us bound to the samsara wheel and separate us from our moksha release. We know our actions and thoughts play a hand in keeping us bound to the world through creating karma, but if we develop practices of discipline, we may have a chance to unite with the divine (or whatever it is) and get off this wheel. We also learned not to take me to the fair.

India and Hinduism have a strong tradition of folks who leave the material world behind to pursue enlightenment and release in caves or forests. Don't confuse these folks with recluses who seek refuge in dark rooms to enjoy the material pleasures of the world as they seek a release from responsibility. We call them teenagers. But maybe you've known folks (or seen pictures of folks) who have forsaken the world of riches and smartphones to pursue the life of true freedom. Maybe you envy them or wish that you had the right stuff to head out there into the world to find your release. Well, it's just not possible for the rest of us to walk away from our responsibilities to seek liberation. Much of the time, my only solitude is in the bathroom. What are we supposed to do? Does any of this stuff have anything to do with our daily lives? How do we even begin to grasp it? Isn't there something in all of this for we who have obligations in this ordinary world? Sure there is. Get ready once again, and I'll show you that you already understand much in this chapter and have plenty of opportunities to get off the Zipper.

1. *Nobody's Atman and Brahman*: Do you believe you have a soul? If not, do you believe you have energy within you? If not, do you believe that things of the world are connected, even socially, and that you play some part? Do you believe that individuals form organic communities that make up the grand society? If so, you are beginning to understand the principle that the great thing is in all things.

Perhaps you've been struggling to find your authentic self. You've tried all kinds of things to be unique, including taking up a quirky hobby or wearing a beret. But then it dawns on you: you don't have to search for that special self. Instead, you simply need to acknowledge it. You decide to take a yoga class or read a holy book to get in touch with something even bigger and more lasting than appearances.

Maybe you take your new awareness into the world. You pull up to a light on your way to the yoga studio and see a person holding a sign asking for money. You feel a tinge of compassion in your gut, realizing that person is you if you didn't have your good job, nice house, loving parents, sturdy genes, understanding friends, two good arms, two good legs, good mental health, or any of your other myriad blessings of life, whatever they are. Perhaps you sense that your two different lives are connected somehow, Atman to Atman. It hits you between the eyes that Atman and Brahman are not far-out concepts for cave-dwelling recluses or the Beatles in 1968 (you know, when they took a break from being a fame-and-fortune-accruing band and went to do Transcendental Meditation with the Maharishi Mahesh Yogi). The whole thing is quite practical. If we are all of one source, or one humanity, then we are all of one community. How you treat others in your daily life says a lot about how others will treat you. When you help me, you are helping you. When you see me, you are seeing you. You can't escape from all that is. One source, one humanity, one community. Just before the light changes, you give the person with the sign a few dollars and realize you are doing yourself a service as well.

2. *Nobody's samsara and moksha*: One night, you take out the trash because it is the right thing to do and not because your spouse asked 200 times. It's the first time in ages no one had to remind you or bother you about it. You realize that taking out the trash is an obligation, and you do it. Period. There's less tension in the house. It feels good. You did the chore without being asked, and it leads to calm in your home. One small release from suffering in this life. You now understand this principle can apply in other settings: the office, the park, or at your place of worship. You become more organized and get tasks done. Suddenly your day and your mind open up a little more. There's less stress at work. More good will in your community. No fight.

The possibility of liberation is in our hands. Even if we can't leave home for the cave in the mountains, we can still take criticism in stride, brake for animals, or cook a meal for our tired spouse who comes home after a hard day without getting huffy about it or expecting a mention in the society section of the newspaper. You see, suffering is often something we create and a cycle we perpetuate. Liberation is a choice to stop creating or participating in it.

3. *Nobody's karma*: Think before you speak. Look before you leap. It's better to give than receive. Yes, these are platitudes, but maybe they're around for a reason. It's true that in some ways of thinking, even good deeds create karma and keep us bound to the wheel. But I'll take my chances. Give a kind word, bite your tongue, be still instead of reacting, don't nag, and pay your debts on time. Be patient. Don't snap at the waiter when your ketchup takes an extra minute. What you do comes back to you. If you have a mean streak, you'll constantly be running into a streak of mean people. What you think has repercussions. Negativity begets negativity. Just watch a trashy talk show for five minutes and pay attention to the interactions between the guests and the audience. How do you feel?

Let me give you an example of how insidious this can be if we're not vigilant. I was driving with my dad up a steep hill, and a driver passed us going about 90 miles per hour in a no-passing zone. He almost killed us. He could have killed someone else. As we came to the crest of the hill, we saw a police car emerge and pull the guy over. Dad and I cheered. We high-fived. We were elated. Finally, justice before our eyes! Now, in this example, where is the bad karma? If you answered, "The jerk in the car that got pulled over saw his actions come right back to him in the form of a speeding ticket," you are correct. If you answered, "The two boneheads in the car celebrating will accrue negative karma for cheering the misfortune of another soul," you are also correct, and shut up. The point is, that guy got his due for almost killing us. However, our celebration at his expense probably will come back on us, as will my calling him a jerk a few sentences ago (thought I missed that, didn't you?). Share the road of life carefully and quietly because it may be me pulled over by the side of the road next time.

4. *Nobody's bhakti yoga*: Do you go to mosque on Friday? Church on Sunday? Do you wake up in the morning with a prayer of gratitude to your selected deity, incarnation, saint, or whatever? If you don't, consider it. No one is asking you to become a renunciant in the Himalayas. Devotion can be as simple as a small remembrance or nod of gratitude.

I have an altar in my room. It's simply a bargain-store stand made of mock bamboo. But upon that altar are assorted items and pictures of wise folks that have special meaning for me. There's no rhyme or reason, just good feeling. I try to give thanks there whenever I can. Am I from the same religion as these figures? No. Am I worshipping the statues and the pictures? No. I'm seeing past the images to the energies that inspired them. I'm peering behind the veil, so to speak. When I honor these great figures, I am honoring the energy they reflect like a clean mirror—an energy that permeates all things. And if I'm wrong about it all? No matter. It makes me feel good, and that good feeling hasn't let me down yet. That devotion gets me out of myself and reminds me that I am part of a bigger feeling and a bigger energy. Everyone looks good in the mirror if eyes are clear.

5. *Nobody's karma yoga*: Go out and play some hoops with the younger neighborhood kids. No, not because you hope they'll someday get an NBA contract and remember the fifty-year-old guy next door when they strike it rich. Do it because it is your duty as an older person to mentor others. Pack a lunch for your wife

before she goes off to work. Not because you are subservient, but because you are in a loving partnership. Write because it's your calling. Sing because it feels right to make the sound. Leave your office door open to your employees throughout the day because you are a manager, and it's your duty to be available. Smile at that guy at church you usually avoid because he has bad breath and corners you at the refreshments table, talking endlessly about his passion for bottle caps. You are at church, and you have a duty to be neighborly and to be loving (remember Jesus's pesky second great commandment?). Uphold what you believe is your highest duty, even in the most difficult circumstances. If you happen to gain wealth and fame from your actions, so be it. If you don't, so be it. Duty is duty.

6. *Nobody's jnana yoga*: Remember the book that woman loaned you? You know, the one about angels? Read it. I know you're a skeptic, but check it out. Watch that television show about ghosts and start forming your own opinions on the matter. Talk to that psychic neighbor who smells like dried flowers (flowers— yeah right!). I know you don't believe in his powers, but maybe he'll surprise you. Challenge yourself with new forms of knowledge. Read the Bible. Read the Gita. Talk with a stranger on the other side of the political rally, and take in his point of view without judgment. Then, take it home and sit alone with it. Open your mind. Meditate on what you find. Try to discover who you really are after you strip away who you think you are. Who knows? You may come to another broad horizon in your life you never imagined could exist.

7. *Nobody's raja yoga*: Stretch in the morning. Pet a dog. Brush your teeth for a third time, even if you're tired and want to fall into bed. Concentrate on your work at work, even if it is boring the living freakin' daylights out of you. Be where you are completely, and learn to focus on the task at hand or the person talking to you.

I know you skipped yoga class this week, but the path is more than postures. Think about ways to improve your health, your thoughts, and your brain. Take yourself seriously so you can wear the royal crown of release.

You see? For all the confusion, you are doing a lot already. And, even if you aren't, you have many opportunities. You have a flesh-and-blood vehicle that can help you achieve all your grandest spiritual goals. Don't forget, this is the only body you have…at least until you die and trade up. Or down. Make the most of it now.

Book of Brahman Meditation

I am all that is. What is in me is the stuff of everything. Help me to find my personal path to unity that can bind me to truth instead of falsehood. May my deeds only bring me closer and closer to union with Brahman. Barring that, please make my next life somewhere with warm temperatures and exotic drinks with those little umbrellas. I think the wheel will spin a little slower there.

NOBODY'S EXERCISES

1. We covered a lot in this chapter. Was there one concept that really struck you? Why?

2. We talked about samsara as a wheel of rebirth born of our attachments and suffering. Is there something in your life that makes you suffer and react? If so, is there some small step you can take to start the process of eliminating it from your life?

3. Many say karma is blind. In other words, it just...is. Have you ever done or said something and wished you could take it back? Did you make amends for it? If not, can you? Would you?

4. Atman and Brahman are intense concepts. Do you agree that the soul in you is a piece of the greater soul? Do you think people are all connected somehow? Can you give an example of this connection from your own life?

5. Fill in the blanks below with ways you think about or do the following. How do they operate in your life?

    Nobody's Atman and Brahman:

    Nobody's samsara and moksha:

    Nobody's karma:

    Nobody's bhakti yoga:

    Nobody's karma yoga:

Nobody's jnana yoga:

Nobody's raja yoga:

Your own meditation:

The Book of Muhammad

Yes, You Can Speak

I will never forget my first university teaching experience. Not the teaching assisting I had been doing in graduate school, but the real deal. I had received a call from my old grad school mentor. He asked if I wanted to teach a course in bioethics, including stem cell research, cloning, abortion, euthanasia—y'know, more of that polite stuff. I jumped at the opportunity. I chose my books (five for under a hundred bucks; beat *that*, other faculty!) and prepared my syllabus, as I had been trained to do. I got all my assignments ready. I even procured one of those old timey grading books and a carrying case for my professorish stuff. I dressed in my best jeans and polo shirt, as I wanted to give off that hip, casual appearance, unlike my undergrad professor who wore the tweed jacket with the leather patches on the sleeves. That's cool, too, I guess, but it's just not me.

I got to the building early. I was prepared. I was ready. I was sweating. I stood outside on a little footbridge and tried to get my heart palpitations under control. I looked down to the ground below at the young students coming and going and thought about when I was in college. I remembered the negative feelings I had regarding certain teachers, and found myself wondering if those profs had noticed. Were they ever scared to teach? Was their confidence just a façade? What was their first day alone in the classroom like?

I was so nervous. Would I know what to say? Would I be able to answer questions? Who would support me in the classroom? There I was, standing out in the sun and trying to get ahold of myself. This was an intense moment. I was so insecure. I eventually sucked it up, found my stride, and went on to accept the nerves as part of the reality of the classroom. It all worked out in the end, and I found that once I started to speak, I loved lecturing.

When I reflect on those first tense moments, I sometimes think about Muhammad. He was a man who also had doubts about what he was going to say. Until he said it.

Muhammad—A Man with a Message

Muhammad (570-632 C.E.) was born in Mecca in modern-day Saudi Arabia. He lost his mother and father early in life, and he lived with his grandfather and uncle. His family was part of the powerful Meccan Quraish—the folks who took care of many important things around the city. These were tribal days, you see, and clans were very important. Muhammad eventually became a caravan driver known for his good character and hard-working nature. At the age of 25 he received a proposal of marriage from Khadijah, a woman 15 years his senior, and for whom he worked. They had a prosperous and happy marriage.

Imagine this young caravan driver Muhammad on the road, making his way here and there. It's very likely he encountered practitioners of other religions of the day, including Christians, Jews, Zoroastrians, and more. A religious studies dream! I like to picture late nights around roaring fires at the oasis. A discussion of gods, ritual, and faraway kingdoms blossoms around hot stew and cool water. Ah, the fantasies of the comparative religion nerd. Nowadays, you're more likely to find young folks discussing religion over leftover pizza in a religious studies department conference room, using tissue as a napkin and plate. Ah, the realities of the comparative religion nerd.

Muhammad himself was a religious man. It is said that he would often go into the caves around Mecca to pray. Then, in 610 C.E., at age forty, something happened. He was praying and meditating when a light came to him and spoke these words (although likely in a much more lyrical Arabic than the translation here):

> Recite thou, in the name of thy Lord who created;-
> Created man from CLOTS OF BLOOD:- Recite thou!
> For thy Lord is the most Beneficent, Who hath taught the
> use of the pen;- Hath taught Man that which he knoweth
> not.[1] (Koran, 96:1-5).

[handwritten margin note: Moses parallel]

An intense experience, no doubt. But how could a man handle such revelation? Muhammad wasn't sure if he heard correctly. Recite? He didn't know what to recite. He wasn't sure what was going on. Luckily, his family was supportive. He told Khadijah of his vision and she felt it was a sign from Allah (God). Over time, Muhammad came to understand his ongoing revelations as gifts from Allah through the presence of the angel Jibreel (Gabriel).

His first disciples were his family and friends. I love that. Isn't it great to know you have that kind of support? I know plenty of people with spiritual curiosity, and they aren't supported, even in their own families. Sad. Not so for Muhammad. Khadijah, Muhammad's friend and father-in-law Abu Bakr, and his cousin Ali were the first to get on board. They called themselves "Muslims" or "ones who submit" (the word "Islam" means "submission"). Muhammad received revelations until his death in 632 C.E. After his death, these revelations were codified in the Koran, Islam's holiest scripture. The Koran is considered the infallible word of Allah. By

[handwritten margin note: Don't we give too much idea...? Compare DIVINE WORD of guide]

the way, although Muhammad is thought to be the final prophet, Muslims consider the Hebrew Testament and the New Testaments of the Bible to contain the words of prophets that came before Muhammad.

During the years of revelation, Muhammad spread messages of justice, care for the needy, and care for children. Pretty great. However, some of his teachings didn't go over so well with the locals. Many folks tried many things to get him to be quiet and to get him out of town. He preached honest dealings in business (including fairness between parties) and, this is a biggie, he preached that only one God—Allah—should be the subject of devotion. Understand that at this time in Mecca, polytheism (belief in many gods) was big business. Pilgrims would come from all around to worship at the Kabah—a cube-shaped building housing religious idols of local tribal gods and goddesses. Folks would make annual pilgrimages to see these. And do business. Starting to see the problem here?

Khadijah died in 619 C.E. Soon after, Muhammad's powerful and protective uncle died. Things were getting hostile around town, and Muhammad began to worry about his personal safety and the safety of his followers. It looked grim until one night, in 620 C.E., when Muhammad had an amazing experience while sleeping outside the Kabah. The angel Jibreel awakened him, and together they rode the legendary horse Buraq from the Kabah to Jerusalem where Muhammad ascended into the heights of heaven. On his way to the highest place, he passed the great figures of the holy books of antiquity: Abraham, Jesus, Moses, Adam, and more. It was on this journey that Muhammad received rules and regulations from Allah, including prohibitions against alcohol and other intoxicating substances, and the direction to pray five times a day. This journey, as story, had the advantage of linking Muhammad to

We have 10 Commandments?

a line of great prophets from other major religions. His special audience with Allah also cemented his stature alongside those figures that had come before him.

This journey bolstered Muhammad and his followers. He knew he was truly a prophet of Allah. Muhammad was for real. Now, things really got hostile. Luckily, men from a nearby city called Yathrib (modern Medina, or "city of the prophet") asked Muhammad to come and adjudicate some issues in their town. Muhammad accepted the invitation in 622 C.E. This event is known as the Hijra, or "migration." This date marks the start of the Muslim calendar because it is the time when Muhammad's message was accepted on a larger scale. Muhammad became a statesman of sorts, and the Islamic community found roots in friendly ground.

The saying that you can't go home again was not on Muhammad's mind. He lived well in Yathrib, but never forgot Mecca. He longed to return and purge the city of its idols. In 630 C.E., he realized that dream. Muhammad and his supporters gained control of Mecca, destroyed the idols in the Kabah, and put their own brand of religious law into effect until Muhammad's death in 632 C.E.

Submit, Give, and Be Well

As we said, a Muslim is one who submits. Islam, then, is the religion of submission. In other words, one submits to Allah. According to the Koran:

> God! There is no God but He; the Living, the Eternal; Nor slumber seizeth Him, nor sleep; His, whatsoever is in the Heavens and whatsoever is in the Earth! Who is he that can intercede with Him but by His own permission? He knoweth what hath been before them and what shall be after them; yet nought of His knowledge shall they

grasp, save what He willeth. His Throne reacheth over the Heavens and the Earth, and the upholding of both bur-deneth Him not; and He is the High, the Great! (Koran, 2:255).

Clear enough? There is only Allah: one, almighty, and all-knowing. Doesn't sleep, knows everything about the doings of people, and upholds heaven and earth without burden(eth).

For devout Muslims, *salat,* or formal prayer, is an essential part of the faith. It is a daily reminder of submission to Allah—a power greater than oneself. It is a way to keep Allah in the fore-front of the mind day and night. Prayer is performed five times per day: before sunup, at midday, midafternoon, just after sunset, and at night. In the Muslim world, the call goes out from the minaret towers, "Allahu akbar!" or, "God is greater!" Then, the call goes on to affirm the creed of Islam that there is no God but Allah and that Muhammad is his prophet. I, for one, would certainly need a call because before sunup, I'm pretty much useless. I have respect for the folks of any tradition who have the commitment and discipline to get up that early to pray.

Before prayer, the devotee gets his mind right and sets a good intention to pray. Then, he goes through a ritual washing of face, hands, and feet as a sign of purification. Often, people pray in groups at the local mosque. Once all are inside and praying, all are equal. Why? Because unlike a movie star in a courtroom, everyone is equal before Allah. Muhammad had a high opinion of prayer, and he believed that it was a gateway for each Muslim to experi-ence what he himself experienced on his Night Journey. I find that particularly amazing. My local city government can't even agree on where to place a gas station, yet a worldwide community of a billion people can rally around one ritual on a regular schedule.

We now know that two of the essentials of Islam are prayer five times per day and that creed I just mentioned above about Allah as God, and Muhammad as Allah's prophet. Something else that binds Muslims is *zakat*, or charity. The purpose of zakat is to care for the poor folks in the community and to take care of the local mosques. The Koran is clear on the important role of charity, saying,

> They who give away their substance in alms, by night and day, in private and in public, shall have their reward with their Lord: no fear shall come on them, neither shall they be put to grief. (Koran, 2:274).

Islam is not the only religious pathway that encourages charity, but what is striking is how central it is. Charity is especially encouraged during the month-long fast of Ramadan. Ramadan is the ninth month on the Muslim calendar, and it marks the time when Muhammad started to receive revelations from Allah. From dawn to dusk the devout avoid food, drink, sex, and tobacco products. Fasting shows complete submission to God. Think about it. If you go for the whole day without food, drink, sex, or an addictive substance like tobacco, it is a pretty good way to show devotion. I'm struggling to remember a time when my day didn't involve sugar! We have so many temptations and diversions in our day. How often do we stop to appreciate a life unmoored from distractions? According to the Bureau of Labor Statistics, Americans aged 15 and over watch an average of 2.8 hours of television per day.[2] That's just television! What about surfing around on the internet, eating junk food, slogging through traffic, texting, playing video games, or sitting around complaining? If we give some of these things up, voluntarily or involuntarily, we may be more apt to consider other things of this world...or above this world. Do you abstain from alcohol? TV? Smoking? Abstention takes discipline, especially if it's something we love or crave. And discipline is a way of showing devotion.

This motif of self-denial for a higher purpose fits in neatly with Islam's other Western cousins, Judaism and Christianity. Jews fast on the day of Yom Kippur, as God commands in Leviticus:

> And this shall be a statute for ever unto you: that in the seventh month, on the tenth day of the month, ye shall afflict your souls, and do no work at all, whether it be one of your own country, or a stranger that sojounreth among you: For on that day shall the priest make an atonement for you, to cleanse you, that ye may be clean from all your sins before the LORD.[3] (Lev. 16:29-30).

Got that? Complete rest on that day, forever, to be cleansed of sins. Including rest for those who happen to be casually sojounething around you. So really, your Jewish friend in school was doing more than just getting out of gym class for the day on Yom Kippur. Once, while taking our laps before class, I overheard a friend tell our high school gym teacher that he was going to be absent for a Jewish holiday. I heard the teacher say to his assistant, "Those Jewish kids get every holiday off!" And yes, that teacher was exactly like the person you're picturing right now.

Christianity has its disciplinary rituals, too. Lent is a time of repentance and self-denial when Christian folks make their spiritual Easter preparations. It's a time when a person can really get inside and think about things. Over Lent, Christians recall Jesus's 40-day period of fasting and temptation in the desert (Matthew 4:1-11).

Though Lent isn't specifically mentioned in the Bible, people take it seriously and often give up something they like. Here's an example from my college days. There was this local bakery that had the best chocolate cake ever. I'm not kidding. I would know. I used to eat a lot of that kind of stuff. In fact, when my family came to visit, we actually got one of these cakes and ate it for days, down to the last rock-hard, stale piece of three-day-old frosting. Anyway, one of my friends loved this chocolate cake, but she also loved Jesus. So, she gave up chocolate for Lent. I felt for her at a birthday gathering for another friend, where one of these giant chocolate cakes arrived. To my friend's credit, she held out. Impressive! I ate a huge piece, but remembered to commend her on her will power. Luckily, she also gave up violence for Lent.

The point is that Islam, Judaism, and Christianity—as well as many other traditions—have fasting and self-denial built right in to show submission, reverence, and discipline. For Muslims, the month-long fast of Ramadan culminates with the feast of Eid al-Fitr. This celebration sees much food and exchanging of gifts and, in one example I know of, younger members of families ask forgiveness from older folks and from each other. I like the idea of times of denial culminating in times of celebration. If life were just about denial, we'd become the kind of people that others avoid, forcing us into an isolation not of devotion, but derision. Denial is also a way to purify for the good times. The times of intimate contact with the holy or divine. Islam has a focus on purity, too. Staying clean is often considered a sign of self-respect and reverence for others. Remember when we discussed cleansing before prayer?

As a counterpoint, I once knew a kid at camp who took pride in being dirty. In fact, his goal was to see if he could make it the whole week without taking a shower. This wasn't one of those clean, indoor camps like NASA space camp or something. It was a camp surrounded by pines, red earth, rocky trails, and shared lavatories. He wasn't in my cabin, so I'm not sure if he succeeded in his messy mission, but I'm sure that if he did, his mother had some choice words for him when he got home.

In that spirit, I have to say there is something special about purification. When I study Islam, I am struck by the attention to purity—the submission to God through cleansing the self. Even the insides of many Mosques are lightly decorated, but exquisitely ornate—evoking an image of purity.

I'm Like Your Friend at Camp. Can I Really Do All This?

These central principles of Islam are simple and powerful. Motivating. They provide a pathway to faith marked by personal and communal devotions. Do we see any of ourselves in this? Is there something for the rest of us in here? How often do we submit to a higher principle? How much do we give? How clean are we who walk this earth in our own traditions? I would argue that we, too, know self-discipline. We know cleanliness. We know purity. Let's see how all of this might play out in action for the rest of us.

1. *Nobody's submission*: A woman is jogging in the park on a crisp, fall day, and she's multitasking—busily talking with her assistant on her cell phone and checking text messages. But in a fleeting moment, she looks up from the trail and notices the amazing view she's earned by the merit of her exercise. She asks her assistant to hold for a moment while she takes it all in. She inhales the fresh air, appreciates the changing leaves, and marvels at the grand spectacle of creation before resuming her busy day. A stressful phone call seems small now in comparison with the grand sky and sweeping vista.

Or perhaps a man gets a rather difficult diagnosis at the doctor's office. His first reaction is one of despair. But then he takes some time to pray and reflect, and realizes over time that there may be more to this situation than meets the eye. He acknowledges the mystery and the plan—whatever it is or wherever it's from—

and starts an online support community to reach out to, and empower, others with his condition and to educate the public on this diagnosis.

Do you give thanks to a creator (if you believe in one), or are your days only filled with the race for more stuff and more doings? Do you make positive change out of mystery, or is there only despair in your unknowns? The famous image of a child kneeling in prayer before bedtime isn't just some Norman Rockwellian throwback. Rather, it is an image of innocence—of submitting the self to something greater. Even if your conception of ultimate power is other than Allah, how often do you bow even your head in reverence to the bigger picture? This question leads us to...

2. *Nobody's prayer*: A man is at work, and the day is getting stressful. The clock hits noon, and the rush is on to get lunch in before the hour is up. He dashes off to get a sandwich and coffee. He returns to his desk and wolfs it down before getting ready to hit the keyboard again. But then he stops. He takes a moment and rolls his neck around. He looks at the picture of his wife and child and says a quiet "thank you" to the universe for making his job worth it. He takes a deep breath. He resets. That night, after he gets into bed, he says another "thank you" to the powers that brought him the warm body breathing quietly next to him.

Or maybe you have a goal to be something or do something. Something to help others or to make your life a little better. Did you know that prayer can also refer to a deep desire or wish? Maybe you don't believe in god, but you can still utter your goal out loud in a quiet moment, breathing life into it and taking the first step to making it real.

Prayer isn't always a public show of penance on parade. Sometimes it's about a silent gratitude or casual thought for someone in need. Have you ever seen a preacher standing on a sidewalk or screaming in a park that this or that person walking by is a sinner? Don't feel guilty that you don't "pray" like that. Take solace in Muhammad's individual revelations in the cave. Or perhaps remember the words of Matthew 6:6,

> But thou, when thou prayest, enter into thy closet, and when thou hast shut thy door, pray to thy Father which is in secret; and thy Father which seest in secret shall reward thee openly.

The loudest voice is often the most insecure. Don't think you need to scream and yell so that god or the universe will hear. Trust me, if it (whatever it is) was powerful enough to bring you forth, it will hear you whether you are in a cave, your closet, or your head.

3. *Nobody's charity*: It's a hot summer day under a merciless sun. You pull up to a light in your air-conditioned car and see a homeless man holding a sign pleading for help (remember him from the last chapter?). You've heard that some people make amazing money in panhandling scams, but you can't bring yourself to believe the downtrodden person at this smog-filled intersection would voluntarily do this. His head is down, and he looks completely done for the day, even though it's only 2 p.m. You check your wallet and find only a few tarnished pennies. You roll down your window and honk the horn. The man looks up. He's heard that sound before, but it was more in a spirit of road rage than charity. He approaches. You grab that extra water bottle from your console and hand it to him. The light turns green, and you pull away before he can say anything. Before you can say anything. You don't need to say anything.

4. *Nobody's fasting*: You were up early and only had a piece of toast before a morning exam. It's now noon, and you're hungry. You get a burrito from the student union and walk by a table on your way out. Your college is having a food drive. They are asking students to miss one meal and donate the food or money to the

drive. The drive workers don't approach you because you are clearly eating, but you reach into your pocket and pull out the buck fifty change from the burrito purchase. You hand it to a woman with a clipboard. She smiles. You eat. Another hungry person somewhere eats. Pocket change brings change.

5. *Nobody's purity*: You are at your place of worship, showered and dressed up in that chic hat you bought when the saleswoman lied to you and told you it was "all the rage in [insert faraway fashion city here]." The services are about to start. On the way to your seat, a friend grabs you by the arm, ready to share a piece of juicy gossip. Do you go in for it? Remember, you are about to pray to your version of the highest good. Can gossip wait for later? Can it wait for never?

Purification isn't only bathing and putting on perfume. It's a sense that you can loosen yourself from old habits and negative thoughts. You know that dirty thing your friend does that annoys you? Well, pick one dirty thing in your own life that you do, stop doing it, then get back to your friend's issues after you've fixed ten more of your own.

If we emerge from our caves to see a world in turmoil, there are small things we can do to make life better. Prayer, charity, self-discipline, and cleanliness aren't just religious tenets for ancient times. Instead, they can enrich our lives today, in this moment. You don't have to take a great journey or be a great prophet to make a difference. Sometimes you just need to be a better part of the community outside your door.

Book of Muhammad Meditation

Let there be a place in my life for surrender, selflessness, charity, and purification. May I use these as powerful tools to help me emerge unscathed from places of doubt. And if I should doubt, may I find support in those closest to me. Barring that, at least help me learn to stop biting my fingernails.

NOBODY EXERCISES

1. Muhammad initially wasn't sure what his visions were. Luckily, his supportive wife and friends helped him out. Have you had a contact with a higher power? An intuition that came true? What was it like?

2. Islam is about submission, or submitting to a higher power. Has there been a time in your life when you just totally surrendered to a situation? To your higher power? Do you need to?

3. The elders of Yathrib took Muhammad in when it looked pretty bleak. He emerged from there stronger and more determined. Has there been a person in your life who has taken you in when you needed it? What was the outcome?

4. Fasting is central to Islam. Have you ever given up something that you loved for the sake of a higher good? What was the result?

5. Fill in the prompts below with an action or thought that exemplifies these amazing features of discipline:

Nobody's submission:

Nobody's prayer:

Nobody's charity:

Nobody's fasting:

Nobody's purity:

Your own meditation:

The Book of Spirit

It's Not All About the Religion

I had a friend in college who used to "go there" with me, conversationally-speaking. We'd have these deep discussions on religion, spirit, and philosophy. I'll never forget late nights with bad booze as the conversations turned more and more obscure. Or maybe we were just tipsy. I don't know. I don't remember so well. Anyway, he once told me that he didn't go to synagogue, even though his Jewish upbringing was very important to him. He loved Moses and the stories from the Bible, but he expressed this love in a different way than many of his peers. I asked what he did instead, and he said he went into nature and prayed. Hard. This drew him close to Judaism, Moses, and the land, even outside the traditional bounds (bonds?) of his religion-by-birth.

I love that image of a person in the wilderness praying with true heart. It reminds me of the days when folks would gather in homes to pray. Or maybe they meditated under a tree like Buddha or sat by a flowing river in a yogic position. Perhaps they did like Muhammad and stole away to the quiet of the cave. They were in deserts. They walked by lakes (or, if they were a certain holy man teaching in Galilee, perhaps they walked *on* them). They were, literally, out there doing it. Many indigenous pathways not covered in this book have close connections with villages and nature, less concerned with endpoints and more interested in cycles and balance. Was my friend any different?

My friend received criticism from folks of many traditions who had their own ideas about how praying *should* be done. Chances are they also had strong opinions on how food should be prepared, how marriages should look, how a piece of clothing should be worn, who should get into heaven, or how the dead should be buried. Of course, if there is ever a zombie apocalypse, that last one will pretty much go out the window and won't those critics have egg on their faces then!

But should we blame the critics? After all, many of these opinions about my friend probably didn't come from anger, but habit. In religion, as in life, we learn from the world outside ourselves and pick up ways of doing things. These ways become habitual. Automatic. When folks don't do it the way we learned, it can be a little off-putting. Maybe we get a little defensive. Is there anything wrong with this? Of course not! We all learn from the outside. It's how we figure out how to tie our shoes, eat spaghetti with a fork, or learn that if we pretend we don't want the last slice of pizza, someone else will kindly insist we take it, thus making us look charitable when in fact we are being manipulative. We learn by watching, taking it in, and then doing it ourselves. Routine can make life easier. Learning by watching helps us grow. When we become attached to certain ways of doing things, it's difficult to encounter a new path or different expression.

The problem isn't the watch-learn-do cycle. The problem arises when we take external cues, internalize them, act on them, and then apply them to others in moral judgment. My friend didn't say he was killing men and eating their flesh, or robbing jewelry stores to use the gems in secret rituals in service to his lord. He wasn't breaking the law in any way. Instead, he was doing something in his own way—following his inner path to personal fulfillment by fashioning his own personal connection with his conception of the ultimate power as he defined it. He had his religion-by-birth and practiced it as a personal-fulfillment-by-design. "I'm not really religious," he would say to me. "I'm more spiritual." You've heard that before, right? If you say no, I'll know you didn't read some of the stuff way back at the beginning. Just say yes.

Your Friend Likes Moses and Is Jewish! Isn't That Religious?

Why do I tell you this story of my friend and his ways? Well, I heard you like the outdoors, so there's that reason. However, it also goes back to that conversation I just mentioned—the one on religion versus spirituality.

Spirituality, like religion, is notoriously hard to define. We said at the start of this book somewhere that spirituality might be considered a subjective, personal feeling or emotion regarding a higher power, or perhaps a personal sense of purpose. Maybe we can think of spirituality as the ultimate pursuit of intensely personal meaning or connection. Maybe it's just the search for the elusive soul. Maybe it's one amazing taste of that chocolate cake we read about before. Let's call spirituality a journey to the center of our personal being that doesn't necessarily require a formal religious outlook.

I have to laugh when someone labels a person's personal faith or spirituality, "bunk." How can you call someone's personal journey or feelings bunk? It's internal. It's particular. It's a subjective call to the self. We can quibble about the wrappers and trappings of religion or the spiritual methods people use to make a connection. However, when it comes to the deep, personal, chocolatey-sweet feelings underneath? Well, that's not so easily swept aside or categorized. For instance, I've known people who tell me they can leave their bodies. They have out-of-body experiences. Should I call that bunk? How the frickity-frack do I know their deep, profound experiences? Am I in their body when they go out of it? Was I there? Did I see it from their firsthand point-of-view? How arrogant to assume that because I wasn't present, it didn't happen. Sheesh. Furthermore, their personal body-leaving ability, whatever it is, has some meaning to them. It is real for them. They are their own measure of proof. And that goes for spirituality, even if not for science or the law. We're not always comfortable with the concept of subjectivity as it applies to others and what they believe. But funny thing—when it comes to our own deeply personal experiences we expect everyone to take us at our word. I'll say it again. Sheesh!

Say my Jewish friend is busy praying somewhere that doesn't happen to be an approved place of worship. Now assume he has a moment of profound connection where suddenly, it (the great "it," the small "it," the it with no quotes...whatever!) all makes sense, even if he is not wearing the prescribed head-covering and no rabbi is present to confirm it. What now? Well, then it certainly seems possible that one can have a profound spiritual experience quite separate from traditional religious affiliation and place of worship. Why is a spiritual connection in synagogue any different than a connection on a dirt path in the middle of the woods?

Some people don't have any religious affiliations. Maybe they just want to improve their life in some way, so they begin the noble quest of personal development divorced from a god, houses of worship, and prohibitions on certain foods and places. They might call that their "spiritual journey." Maybe they read about Confucius and are trying to be a better parent or partner, or perhaps they like to meditate quietly on some of the Buddha's teachings. Can't that be spiritual, too? There's nothing at all wrong with formality, rules, prescribed rituals, and holidays. And there's certainly nothing at all wrong with a more informal approach that brings the same peace. Maybe that's the essence of spirituality.

But then we have *religion*—that pesky word that gets us into so much trouble. Hard to define? Yeah. We covered that already. Pages ago. When we look at the "religious" as opposed to the "spiritual," we can think of religion as the formal end of spirit, or the formal institution that tries to foster a sense of spirituality. There are external rules and regulations and, often, a hierarchy of administrators or mediators of a god, gods, or knowledge. I guess the idea is that through formal worship and structure a sense of personal spiritual emotion will arise.

However, what about a person that stands in a formal house of worship without the slightest twinge of spiritual feeling? Take my friend for example. He feels connected when he is outside praying. He may go to synagogue, but that is not where he feels connected. One could say, then, that he belongs to a religion on a social and cultural level (he likes Jewish jokes and food), but that his spirituality is located somewhere else (did you hear the one about the Jewish guy who goes into the woods to pray?).

There is a strong feeling in my close circle that spirituality is something we can access through formal channels or on our own initiative. If one comes from a religious background, there may still be favorite foods and holidays, but the dogmatic trappings aren't necessary to engender unity and good feeling. Take my friend again. He believed religion should respond to a growing need for spirituality—going beyond prescription and description and entering the arena of emotion and expression. Many people don't necessarily want to choose between their religion-by-birth and their spirituality-by-choice (though some do). Instead, seekers are getting the sense that they can bring their matzo balls to the forest, and eat them too.

I Want That Whole Religio-Spiritual Thing, but I'm Not Sure Where to Start!

There is liberation in acknowledging the spiritual as something one can pursue either separate from or connected to religion. In other words, you can have both. You can find something new and invigorating in something ancient and stable, or you can leave the latter behind. This realization frees up lots of space inside. Think about it. Once you give up the guilt of not doing this ritual or that prayer the way you were told, and you acknowledge that it's okay to have your own feelings separate from, or in addition to, formal structure, you can really get cracking. Check your religion's archives, and I'll bet you'll come up with a saint or visionary insider who had an amazing sense of personal connectedness while working within the religious structure. Hey, what can stop you now? And by the way, this isn't only for the religious or spiritual seeker. If you're part of a society and you participate in formal social structures, and you want to do something new or different, then feel free to participate!

But how do we begin? How do regular folks like us figure out how we feel about the heavy and intense topics in this book so that we can turn them into something useful on our path? How do we get down and dirty with ourselves and find true honesty about all the religious, spiritual, and other potentially life-changing things in our lives? It all seems too big! It all seems so overwhelming! Where's the remote? I need a distraction!

Hold on. Come back to the table, please. Actually, the whole thing is quite simple. You are who you are in this moment, with all your habits, limits, tastes, and fears. However, you also have the capacity to learn, search, and sort. Start the spiritual journey, or whatever kind of journey you want to call it, by taking stock of where you are now. Are you in a religion? Not in a religion? Seeking a new form of expression in the secular world? Looking to improve your life? Already on the path? Completely apathetic and sick of my incessant questioning? It doesn't matter. Start from here. Start from now.

Next, take notice of new ideas to see how they fit into your ongoing life. Do they enrich or enliven you? If yes, study them a little more. If not, discard them. We do this all the time, although it has become hidden behind routine. Don't believe me? Well, let's use the house/home example again.

When we look for a place to live, we want to find the dwelling that feels like home to us, even when our families and realtors who don't have to live there weigh in with their opinions. We had preferences and a style before the formal search began, but now we're more in tune because we're serious about finding our own personal, perfect place to live. We're on the journey. We're more conscious. We pay more attention when we're on the real estate website or in a design store. We become open to new ideas. We watch that cable show where people see three homes and pick one (note: it's usually the wrong one). We learn some stuff. We list out must-haves and deal-breakers. We may have grown up in a split-level, but now we want a Craftsman or ranch style. One bathroom worked for our family of 10 growing up, but now two would be nice. We look at homes through our new lens, take stock of our options, and pick the one that fits our personal notion of "home" as we now define it. You research and evaluate jobs, partners, pets, and cars in great detail. Why not take inventories in the spiritual or social life as well? Start from where you are, but then expand. Open. Search. Pay attention. Ask your own questions and look for your own answers. Pick what feels right.

Let's assume you were born into a religion, but you're thinking of doing some exploring now. If you're not religious, then consider your place in society and whether you'd like to change it up. You've asked some of the preliminary questions, figured out my wandering housing metaphors, and decided to take things to the next step. What would that look like? Well, start with a central question. In our previous example, this could be, "What does 'home' mean to me?" Spiritually or socially, this can take the form of anything meaningful to you on your path with which you want to be in greater touch. There are no spreadsheets or formal rules in this self-improvement inventory. Just a checklist of feelings. It's a simple thought exercise to figure out where you stand now and to get a baseline, so the stakes are only as high as you want them to be. You can stop betting any time you want, and you can't fail. Nice, right? For instance, start with a really big, super-colossal question: "What is my conception of the highest power or greatest principle?" Is it a bearded man in the sky? An animal spirit that you treasure? A code of ethics? Something else? Is it nothing? That's great, too. See where the answer takes you. Up? Down? Right where you are? Left at the intersection? To the kitchen for a snack? Go where you want. See the sights inside. Study. Sit. Think. Feel.

Next, if you are a religious kind of person (or not), you might think about how you feel at your place of worship in relation to that power or principle. If you're not religious, think about how existing social structures support what you believe. Really get into it and pay attention. Are you calm? Agitated? Serene? Victimized? If your conception of god, higher power, or highest principle differs from your religion's or society's point of view, do you feel like an outsider? Empowered? Indifferent? Any word will do because they're your words. Are you closer to connecting when you're at the ocean? In the desert? In the mall? Do you need to break away from a social habit and strike out on your own path?

Okay, so you've thought about what higher power or a higher principle means to you, and you've considered how you feel when worshipping or thinking about that power or principle in relation to your religion or structured social system. Next, consider whether your religion or social structure supports your conceptions and feelings. If not, is there a branch of your tradition or social group that would support it? In my friend's example, he believes Orthodox Judaism is too restrictive and has too many rules, regulations, and prohibitions. Fine. That's his opinion. But he has found other streams of Judaism that are closer to his point of view. If you have a strong tie to a religious pathway or social system that doesn't support your point of view, and you feel unsatisfied, is there a way to supplement your formal attendance or social obligations with something more personalized? Have you considered a community lecture or a class? Does that feel right to you? Would you like some additional enrichment? Is that what's lacking? Do you need to seek out friends who share and support your interests? Perhaps you don't have to toss out your heritage or abandon society altogether. Maybe there's a way you can honor tradition *and* a fresh approach. My friend has carved a niche in Judaism. He loves his tradition, and he loves his personal spiritual expression. That's a good balance.

All this inventorying is a way of gut checking. In other words, you are starting with a question of great significance and asking yourself important questions about how you feel at each stage of the search. You're also staying open and exploring other concepts. A question about how you feel at church on Sunday could lead you to more volunteering, a spiritual retreat in Colorado, a yoga class, or a quiet walk with your dog while you count your blessings with each step you take. Better yet, count them with each step your dog takes. That way, at his pace on four legs, you'll be giving thanks for a bazillion more things. Nothing horrible is going on in this inventory. Nothing judgmental. Just you checking in with you and trying some stuff out to find a good fit. You don't have to be religious or spiritual to do it. You could just be a person looking for a new way forward in society. Take a friend. Go alone. It doesn't matter. Think of it this way: with all the different religious, spiritual, and philosophical pathways in the world, the highest power (whatever it is) is sure trying out a bunch of different stuff in a bunch of different forms. Why should you miss out on the fun? And hey, if you're happy right in the house where you are, this exercise will show you that, too.

I want to mention another step you might like: keeping a journal. You're doing a version of journaling at the end of each chapter in this book, and that's by design. Journaling can be very liberating, and it's a great way to own your experiences. I know you've heard this advice before from your therapist or favorite talk show, but it's sound. Journal your experiences on this personal-growth quest so that you can keep track of what goes on inside of you. Emotions and thoughts can get lost amid other details, like pennies in the cushions. But you can grow rich if you keep them close and save them dutifully. Did you go to Mass on Sunday? How did you feel? Invigorated? Good. Jot that down. Then, after you and your friend get back from yoga, and you've taken a few painkillers and are now icing down your sore spots, jot down that feeling. Rearrange the furniture in your bedroom to facilitate good energy flow. Forget the cynics. Do it because you're curious about *feng shui*. How do you feel after a few days in your new digs? Write it out. At the end of a week, month, or year, take a look at the results while you sip some green tea and eat a sugar-free cookie. What emotions come up around your religion? What new insights do you have about your personal spirituality? How do you feel now about being in your social circle? How are you feeling? Brighter? Darker?

Lighter? Weighed down? More connected? Less connected? Achy? Ready for the nunnery? Ready to send your daughter to the nunnery? Write it down. And if you hate writing? Well, just take mental notes.

Here's another tidbit: the stuff on your path (and in your journal) is for you. You don't need to share it around, and you certainly don't owe anybody anything. This is *your* spirit or calling we're talking about, and it animates *you*. It's your feelings we're interested in, not your friend's—you know, the one who scoffs at your experiments. If you do meet resistance from others, and it's creating a block on your path, supplement your social life with more supportive people and groups. It may take some courage, but what worthwhile project doesn't? Not everyone will agree with you, but then again, not everyone will deride you. Do what feels right. Change it up. Change friends. Change you. If the Buddha's right, you might have another chance in your next lifetime, so take a risk in this one. Get creative. Once the tap comes on, all kinds of awesome things pour out. And if brown, smelly stuff flows? Turn it off and try a different tap.

Easier said than done? Sure. But you spent years getting addicted to cigarettes, learning the opening riff to Stairway to Heaven on guitar, and perfecting that awful Richard Nixon imitation that your family dreads at parties. You frittered away ages picking out carpet and drapes to match Aunt Sadie's ugly hand-me-down candy dish that your spouse wants to smash. You went on plenty of forgettable dates to find that one person with whom you could connect. And how about all the Saturday afternoons it took you to find that picture in the guest bathroom? You know, the one with the creepy clown that no one has the guts to say they hate even though they have to sit there and stare at it because you don't have any good magazines next to the toilet. That took a while to find. Why shouldn't your search for spirit, inner peace, and knowledge matter as much?

Are You Sure This Spiritual Search Is Okay? All Those Religions Can't Be Wrong, Can They?

I don't claim to know what comes after this life. I don't have all the answers to a better tomorrow. Heck, some people would say I don't have any answers. But the religious pathways we've covered in this book certainly claim to have some of the answers. And as we've seen, some of their central teachings are applicable to us right now in our own lives, just waiting to help us improve and feel better. But you should remember that much in religion is subject to interpretation. Much is subject to point of view. I like to think that had I been present at some of those early councils and meetings where a bunch of dudes (yes, usually and unfortunately, dudes) got together to hash all of this religion stuff out, I might have voted differently. I would have voted for more female presence in the religious sphere of influence or to include different foods on the "prohibited" list (hint: green peppers). I might have argued that the role of geography in religion shouldn't dictate lives for generations to come. After all, if the Hebrews had fled from France, there would probably be a central place at the Passover *seder* for puff pastry and baguettes instead of matzo.

But one day I realized something. I live in a time and place where I can vote differently. My karma (for good or ill, I'm still not sure) has put me in a position to study traditions, take account of the new, re-fashion the old, and find a center. Not *the* center. *My* center. Not a center approved by scientists that I can objectively share and thus make real for spectators. Not a center that cynics would like or accept. Not a center that has someone else's definitions. It's all mine. Blasphemous? I don't think so. Risky? Maybe. Popular? Not always. Worth it? Totally worth it.

To give you a little motivation, and to show you that it is possible to carve out your own niche in this endless search, here's the tally from my evolving journey: I'm a boy from the U.S.A. who loves to study religion, spirituality, and practical philosophy. I have a deeper appreciation for my birth religion now than I did when I was younger. I meditate in a yoga lineage descended from an Indian saint, and I have statues of the Buddha in my room right next to the Prayer of Saint Francis and the Jewish *hamsa* someone got me to ward off the evil eye. Or for good luck. Or something like that. Whatever it is, it's great. I say my mantras throughout the day, utter some prayers at night, and basically, I just go with it. I'd lunch with Jesus in a heartbeat if the opportunity arose, and I would be more than happy to extend that invitation to Moses, Confucius, and Lao Tzu, assuming he could catch an ox going my way. My bookshelf looks like a religious studies department had an everything-must-go sale. I have spiritual teachers from different traditions who teach the same beauty, and I never think I can't learn more and have more insights. Anyone could be my instructor and anyone could be my student. We're all just folks trying to make it out there, and we should be sharing whatever we can when it comes to personal growth because it's the one thing in the world (besides love) that can never be wasted.

I'm a work in progress. You're a work in progress. The world is a work in progress. As long as your search doesn't harm others, then go in peace. Life's too short and eternity's too long to wait.

I'm Still Confused and Stuck on Definitions (Didn't We Cover That Millions of Pages Ago?)

I can still hear a few of you out there saying, "I'm so confused! Religion? Spirituality? I still don't get it!" I know a lot of folks feel that way. I feel that way. Maybe you read that preceding section (or this whole book) and got all lost in figuring out the labels. Sometimes people get bent out of shape if someone suggests they aren't "good" Christians or "traditional" Buddhists, even though no one really knows what all of that means. People may feel flustered if their personal spiritual practices are defined by others as "weird." People insist that "spiritual" and "religious" are either empty of meaning or else too full of themselves as categories. Definitions, definitions, definitions. Good lord.

Listen to me. Like you, I struggle with definitions. That's why I talk about them in this book over and over. I often get caught up in the idea that unless I really get a concept from all angles, I don't have permission to progress. I read and research something, then I do it all over again. That's great when we're arguing a case to the Supreme Court, doing heart surgery, or making investments. But when it comes to the spirit or our own personal growth, definitions tend to suck us in and keep us bound to the ground. At a certain point we must reach an escape velocity and start the business of soaring.

The journey of personal fulfilment is a journey beyond words—to defy definition. It's a journey back to your authentic self each and every day, right in the everyday world. It's a journey of world and personal healing, and permission to change. Words and definitions in this context are just glitzy neon, blinding us to deeper meaning. Never forget that. If it's a hot day and you pass a convenience store with a flashy sign for some soft drink brand in the window, it's not the sign that gets you in the door. It's what the sign represents: the feeling of a soda sating your thirst on a sticky, sweaty day. You must feel the sensation of thirst before the sign can speak to you, otherwise it's just decoration. Strive to experience spirit before you define it. You can find your center, and you know what "center" means to you, with no definition required. You know how to heal your emotional wounds, and you know how to heal the world. You understand what "authentic" means, even though an expert who doesn't see the irony will tell you your definition is wrong. You already know how to connect to what's most important every day, even if you can't swat it with a dictionary. You are already on the path! You inspire! Are these exclamation points convincing you?!! Maybe the following spiritual principles will!

1. *Nobody's world and self-healing*: Do you put your empty bottles in a recycling bin? That's a contribution to helping the earth. Do you call for calm when others are hysterical? That helps society in ways you can't imagine. Have you let go of old practices and toxic people that don't serve you anymore? That brings peace and clarity beyond measure. Maybe you've donated clothes, cleaned up your space, patched up a friendship with an apology, or done something nice for someone in the neighborhood. When you do for others, you do for yourself. But you also do for the world. And that's got to lead to feeling good. "Healing" is whatever you want it to be.

2. *Nobody's connection to the inner self in the everyday*: I once visited a place in Utah called the Valley of the Gods. It's so isolated, it's almost creepy (but it isn't). My brother and I drove into the heart of this amazing place that is filled with stone monuments and dust. We parked, got out, and slammed the car doors shut behind us—the sound echoing into an insane eternity. We stood still. It was so absolutely quiet, my eyes watered. I imagine that is the nature of pure inner connection. I know we can't be in that state

of silence all the time, but do we at least try to connect with our still, quiet core when things are out of sorts? Do we remember to stop and take a moment? Do we eat a favorite health food when we're not feeling good, or journal our thoughts when we need to take stock of our lives? Perhaps we do a breath technique that resets the mind. Maybe she scrapbooks or he goes swimming. Do what you need to do out there to get in touch with what you need to touch in here.

There are hundreds of tapped and untapped ways to reconnect with what is most precious and most important inside of you. It's not definitions and rules that get you back to your source, but the intentions and good will behind what you do. At the end of the day, the question is not how far you've drifted from your core, but how you commit to return. Hell, we all stray. But do we focus on heading home again?

Book of Spirit Meditation

Let me keep my own counsel on religious definition. Let me mold the lump of clay that is my personal spirituality. Let me enjoy both—or neither—as my conscience dictates. Bring me easy and fruitful dealings with my fellow humans. Guide me to those things most healthy for my soul, and keep me from that most toxic to the spirit. And, if I happen to be surrounded by the toxic things in my life, let me have a phone with caller ID and my own room with blessed door and lock for ease of escape.

NOBODY'S EXERCISES

1. Have you ever said, "I'm more spiritual than religious"? If so, what does that phrase mean to you? What is "spiritual"?

2. Do you have a spiritual or religious practice that you created or that goes against the "norm" for your community? How did it develop? Do others accept it?

3. Is finding your "center" important to you? Whether or not you believe in a soul makes little difference. A boat has an anchor. A tetherball has a...tether—even when it is batted around like hell, it stays close to the pole. What are some activities you can pursue, or do pursue—such as yoga, journaling, meditation, or exercise—that might keep you a little more grounded and stable in a world of change and occasional hardship?

4. Fill in the prompts below with examples of how you heal in the everyday and how you find that inner connection every day. Remember, your connections are your business, and it is up to you to decide how to personalize them.

Nobody's world and self-healing:

Nobody's connection to the inner self in the everyday:

Your own meditation:

The Book of Socrates

If It's All Greek to You, That's Fine by Me

No conversation around religion and spirituality would be complete without a discussion of doubt, proof, and—yes—a world where we can improve without religion. Yeah, we've alluded to these things in other chapters, but I think we should bring it all together. In that spirit, let's devote a book to some of those tough themes. I'd like to start off with a classic phrase that I'm sure is as old as religion itself. It's a tried-and-true answer to life's most earnest and difficult questions. It's a pithy six-word gateway to ultimate freedom. Ready? Here it is: "Because I said so, that's why!"

Don't you just love that phrase? I know you like to use it, just not to hear it. It's the bane of existence for so many children. Whenever I hear it, I think it must have roots in some secret society of parents. Maybe in 1700s England a group of exasperated adults got together and held a secret meeting in some room they rented from the Masons or something. They sat down and had a long discussion on the merits of concocting a phrase that would shut down a kid's questionings and whinings.

"I'm tired of little Johnny not putting down the hoop and stick when I ask him!" yells one mother.

"William won't shoe the horses when I tell him to," shouts a man from the back. "He keeps asking why he has to do that instead of playing in Farmer Finnegan's mud hole with the other children."

A man with a beard and wig bangs a gavel at the front of the room.

"Silence all! Silence. I have a solution." An excited mumble ripples through the crowd. "We must simply emphasize to children they have to do something because we say so. In that way, we can stifle their natural tendencies to curiosity and wandering, and buy ourselves a few extra seconds of peace each day. Imagine it! Over the span of your adult life, you will have minutes and minutes of extra time. Of course, when your life expectancy doubles in a few hundred years, that will mean twice as much."

A child's questions can be frustrating to adults because we want kids to just...*get it.* Adults know that using an inside voice in a restaurant is proper. Therefore, when a three-year-old wants to scream in a restaurant and then asks why he can't after you "shush" him, it is frustrating to have to explain why it's not appropriate. Then again, sometimes explanation isn't necessary. When my brother and I misbehaved, and Mom wanted us to stop, there wasn't a whole lot of discussion or questions. She abandoned logic and brandished her famous wooden spoon that never touched us. It simply had to be produced. No questions asked.

Billy Returns! (Or, How Adults Get Around Kids Like Billy.)

Let's once again make an appeal to the great sage we've met so many times in this book: Billy. Remember Billy? He's the kid who kept peppering us with questions. Billy is simply doing what comes naturally to children: attempting to get to the root of all things by, quite literally, asking every question that comes to mind with no cessation. Just pure flow. That is natural in the child's mind in the moment. He isn't interested in seemingly definitive answers or pretenses to knowledge. He doesn't think about re-specting a person's sanity or day off in front of the game with a cold beverage and a handful of tortilla chips. It's just about the questions. Indeed, if left unchecked, Billy would ask every question in the world. Until the end of life. Until the earth careens into the sun. Why? Children have agendas of their own. Children want to howl in libraries and eat ice cream for breakfast. If you say an activity is inappropriate, they want your reasons. Children are naturally curious. Children want to know.

When adults are in conversation with other adults (and, sometimes, with children), and they don't have an answer to a deep, personal question, they can: (1) make answers up; (2) rely on someone else's conclusions and answers and provide those—even if they're not entirely accurate; or (3) say "I don't know" and investigate further. (Note: the wooden spoon approach, which in this list would be approach number four, is the most efficient. But we'll skip that one for now.) I find that choice number one works well in a pinch, but it isn't ultimately that satisfying. It's also probably really lousy karma. Choice two is convenient, but it doesn't get us very deep. It's fine for general knowledge questions or when citing scientific studies. But when it comes to personal stuff, it's not the best way to go. I mean, do we really want to parrot an answer that some talking head gave about his or her own personal life? If we don't have the research or reasons behind an answer, then someone is eventually going to call our bluff and we'll look twice the fool. As for choice number three? Well, three requires us to admit our ignorance and then go home and do some digging. Number three takes courage and is a choice that we like to pretend doesn't exist, especially when we're trying to impress some stuffed shirts at a networking meeting. Or a kid with a sucker stick hanging from his mouth.

When it comes to investigating religious traditions, searching for our own authentic spirituality, or pursuing any kind of growth or self-improvement in the world, which approach should we take to the difficult questions? Should we make stuff up? Use other people's answers? Can we just say, "Because I said so, that's why!" when someone is genuinely trying to question and investigate our beliefs? That phrase may work when assigning chores, but when we get to the ultimate questions of life, it just isn't very satisfying. We're not talking about definitions again, mind you. We're getting into the business of really standing in our beliefs, whatever they are.

For a lot of folks, the jury is still out on many of the relevant questions of God, gods, spirit, karma, church, keeping kosher, avoiding alcohol, and whether or not to move to Jerusalem. The jury will likely be hung for eternity. Are the figures and founding events of many beloved traditions absolute products of flesh and blood history, or are they an amalgam of person, place, idea, and myth? Are the gorgeously scintillating texts we hold dear divinely inspired messages from divine source and mystical intuition, or simply wonderful works of prose and poetry composed at the hand of talented scribes throughout history? Is this particular ritual really necessary? Is that prayer only for this place of worship? Even in non-religious contexts we ask hard questions. Should I strive for change or adhere to expectations? Will society accept my point of view? What if I'm rejected for my new way of thinking? Should I pursue personal growth or just find comfort in how I am right now? We want answers. Real answers. Lasting answers.

As times, politics, and tastes change, opinions change and doctrines shift and sway. They must, or they'll fade. What was prohibited yesterday may be more acceptable today. Women are now rabbis in some streams of Judaism; in 1517, Martin Luther spearheaded a split of Catholic and Protestant branches of Christianity;

and the Second Vatican Council under Pope John XXIII in 1962 led to more open and inclusive policies, including using local languages in some church services. Not all Muslim women wear a headscarf, and not all Hindus are vegetarian. Some Jewish people cover their heads, some don't. Some eat pork, some won't. The answers to the tough questions change things on the religious and spiritual path. And sometimes, people create answers even without asking questions.

Aren't We All a Little Bit Billy?

TRADITIONAL RELIGIONS have appeal to this type

Religious and spiritual dialogue is starting to reflect Billy's need-to-know attitude as more and more followers are asking the powers that be the great question of youthful innocence: "Why?" And "Because I said so!" just isn't going to cut it. That third choice of saying "I don't know," and investigating further, is making headway.

When it comes to our own pursuits on this path—religious, spiritual, or secular—what are we to do with this messy business of proof and others wanting to know our motivations? People may ask us, "Why are you meditating? What good is that gonna do?" Or they may say, "You're on a self-improvement kick? That's so '90s! Aren't you afraid of what people will think? You're not joining a cult, are you?" We may even begin to doubt our own practices because skeptics (or, more properly, cynics) constantly bombard us with questions about those practices. We may have good answers for ourselves, but what if others don't accept those answers? We don't have to give an answer, true, but some of us feel compelled to provide one, especially to those we love. We want to defend what we believe. To justify it. Or perhaps we want to hear ourselves say something out loud to prove to ourselves that the things we do to grow and improve are real. Proof is powerful because it

What would you tell a scientologist tells us it's okay to spend our personal or spiritual currency in certain ways. It answers questions so that things can be settled.

The issue of proof can have very real consequences, and the issue certainly won't ever go away. Someone is always going to tell you your beliefs or pursuits aren't grounded in anything other than wishes, dreams, and myth, and that can bring us down or put us on the defensive. If you are one of those folks who tells someone their religious or spiritual way is bunk (please don't say it that way), you are likely to rest at least one of your arguments on the grounds that no one can prove the existence of God, miracles, energy, spirit, or an interconnected web of whatever. But that's not fatal to the personal search. Why? I've told you why: the individual is the measure of his or her private religious and spiritual experiences. The person is the measure of his or her growth. That may not apply to parole boards or psychiatry, but it must apply in the domain of personal growth and spiritual and religious experience. Let me share a story with you. And yes, let me assure you at the outset, this happened.

Years ago, as a new law grad, I couldn't find a way to resonate with the legal profession. My whole life had led to that law degree, so I tried. I did. I worked for some really nice folks (and some really not nice folks) and did some good work (and some yucky work), but just couldn't bring myself do it anymore. I'd go to conferences and listen to folks ramble on about this or that law or statute and how to work it this or that way, and I just couldn't bear to listen to it anymore. Many in the room loved it. I didn't.

I shared these concerns with folks in my life who just couldn't bear to listen to *me* anymore, and urged me to seek guidance. This was a huge issue for me. But for them? No. One evening I found myself seated across from an influential teacher in my life. He said that I could ask a question. Well, a head too full of questions of every shape and size moments before suddenly drew a blank. I simply asked, "Should I stay in the law?" The teacher regarded me for a moment and said, "You know, it's only work." Then he turned to a picture of Babaji, a great saint and yogi of India, on a desk to his right. He asked if I knew who it was, and I acknowledged that I did. Taking match in hand, my teacher lit a candle in front of Babaji. Then he said, "I'm going to ask that you receive a message that work is only work." In other words, that I am myself, separate from my occupation. That a job is often a means to other ends if it cannot be an end in itself. This was all very nice, but I was upset and embarrassed about this whole thing. It felt wrong to have a problem that people often don't consider a problem, so even when good advice came my way, I wasn't that receptive. I was more in a "Whatever!" kind of mode.

A few days later, my phone rings. It's Dad. Dad never calls. It's always Mom (of course) who checks in. Anyway, Dad said, "Hey, I just had the weirdest experience. I was in the back office at my desk and a man's voice just spoke to me and said, 'Call your son and tell him it's only work.' Does that mean anything to you?" I was stunned silent. He then went on to tell me that the house was quiet and that he didn't know where the voice came from. After regaining my composure, I told him about my experience.

That story binds us as father and son. It unites us on our paths apart and together. When I find my faith (such as it is) waning in grim shadow, I remember the gift of that event when it all came together in an event one usually only reads about in musty books. My problem was my problem. It was real to me. And my pursuit of an answer led to an event that has kept me going on the search even when I want to quit. I'm nobody in particular, but I can still have life-changing moments. We all can.

So, proof. Are Dad and I losing it? Do you believe this event occurred? I've told this story to many, as it has become part of my personal lore. And trust me, it isn't always received well, especially by those who feel that if they weren't personally present in my life to witness it, then it doesn't have the ring of authenticity. I don't blame them. In fact, I praise the skepticism because I know that all spiritual experiences are a version of: *if a tree falls in the forest and no one is around to hear, does it make a sound?* My detractors weren't in the forest with my family that evening, so this experience may not make a sound for them. But if they demand proof, and I can't provide it, does it negate the experience? No way! Should I judge another's experience and demand proof? No, unless we are making government policy, seeking scientific breakthroughs, or fashioning a research study. Will screaming and yelling that a person is wrong accomplish anything? I'm guessing no.

You certainly have every right to disagree with a person's belief system, spiritual outlook, or path to self-improvement, but chances are your continued and insistent disagreement won't get any work done. I may not like how you view the world or other people, but telling you that likely won't change your mind. In fact, it would be arrogant for me to think I have things all figured out to the point where I can freely share my opinion and judgments on the lives of billions of fellow travelers. Maybe it's best if I just say, "I don't know your motivations or your deepest thoughts. And I don't know the answer to everything. I disagree with you, but perhaps since you're not hurting anybody, I should just let you go in peace to pursue your own vision." I don't have to approve or condone. I do have to pause and be respectful, and allow you to pursue your vision of the good life—whether or not you have proof. Sometimes admitting we don't know is the surest path to satisfaction. It frees us up to walk away, investigate, form our own conclusions, and live a more authentic life. It allows others to do the same.

 Ask questions. Take in answers. Seek your own path. Maybe Billy is on to something.

The Gadfly in the Ointment

Perhaps Socrates (470 B.C.E. - 399 B.C.E.) should weigh in here. You remember Socrates, right? He was the great gadfly of ancient Athens that no one could shoo away. He was the thorn in the side of the establishment, exposing the self-styled greats as ignorant folk. He was the guy who hung around in the ancient agora and called influential people out on their pretenses to knowledge, which of course led to his death. He took philosophy to the streets. I just had to include him in this book because, for one thing, he's too awesome not to. But also, when it comes to aspiring to the highest values, examining the good life, and getting to the core of belief, there's no more committed figure in history.

As far as we know, Socrates came from regular people just like you and me. His father was a stoneworker and his mother, a midwife. I've always found that fascinating because when I think of Socrates, I think of a man who chiseled away layers of ignorance to expose raw truth, as well as a teacher who attended the birth of so many insights. He fought in the Peloponnesian War, and was known as a man of great courage. He was just a guy who did his duty for Athens, and did it well. His home life is a different story, but that's another book.

Anyway, Socrates couldn't get enough of the good ol' philosophizing (my computer tells me that's a word, so I'm going with it), and he is a founding figure in the study of ethics. In a device now known as the Socratic method, he asked people question after focused question to get to the core of truth and to root out problems and inconsistencies. It's a dialogue. A way of getting the thought motor running. The questions are intended to elicit our true values. There's no "expert" lecturing you from a podium. It's a two-way search. Sound fun? It can be. But it can also be a little...shall we say...uncomfortable.

Imagine you're a self-professed artist, teacher, and maker of "beautiful things" in ancient Athens, selling your wares and your expertise. Socrates perhaps would be nearby, asking a crowd, "What is beauty?" You have some time to kill, and maybe you're not smart enough to keep your trap shut, so you volunteer to answer. Socrates says, "You fancy yourself an expert in beautiful things, and I would so much like to learn about beauty." If you were now a little smarter, you would collect your wares and run like Hades. However, being a confident "expert," you would engage him. Perhaps you answer that beauty is a state of things in the world that brings joy to the viewer. Then, as you were making to leave, Socrates would follow up on his first question with other questions (I warned you!), putting your assumptions around "beauty" and "joy" to the test. He'd find exceptions or limits to your answers and get you all good and bothered. After a short time, you'd find yourself contradicting your previous answers and slogging through the bogs of your own ignorance. Then your blood would boil a bit and you might discover you were no expert to begin with. Fine. You might shake hands and move on with your day, or you might belt him in the yapper. Although, I suppose you could do both.

Now imagine you are a great general or a senator. You're standing in the agora and talking about your views on bravery, government, and all sorts of mighty topics. It all sounds impressive, and folks are joining the crowd, eager to hear your words. Socrates arrives on the scene and asks a question about proper governance or your views on courage in the battlefield. He isn't angry or anything. He doesn't fancy himself an expert on this stuff. He's just skeptical. He wants to know more about what's behind your words. Are your mansions of values built on stone or sand? You answer with confidence. He counters with more questions. You counter. Then you realize your definition falls short. How do you feel now? Exposed? Embarrassed? Cowardly? Like I said, his inquiries led to his death. He should've stopped with artisans.

The joy of Socrates is his (false?) humility. See, he claimed the only thing he knew was that he knew nothing, even though others claimed he was a man of special brilliance. Instead, he believed it was his method of honest and penetrating interrogation that could draw truth out of a person, or at least expose shortcomings in a person's assumptions. He was a digger and an explorer—an archaeologist uncovering truths by way of a slow, methodical shovel. Years ago, when I was digging at an archaeological site, I knew that I didn't build the buildings or mint the coins whose remnants peeked through the dirt. I was simply applying a tool that drew these ancient pieces from the ground. I polished the uncovered treasures, catalogued them, and shared them, but I didn't actually create them. It was the same with Socrates. He wanted to unearth the truth on the nature of beauty, wisdom, and the good life, and he wanted an honest dialogue that could be polished and admired. He wasn't making the truth. He wanted to uncover the truth. Socrates wanted to fight ignorance and discover the good life. He wanted to know how we *ought* to act and be. Socrates set a high standard. He poked, prodded, and pushed. He gained friends, foes, and infamy.

His many enemies finally succeeded in bringing him to trial on trumped up charges of corrupting the youth and not having faith in the gods of Olympus. Socrates knew these charges were unjust, and he maintained his virtue through the trial. His persecutors expected him to throw himself down and beg for mercy, but he didn't. They expected he might run away, retire to the seashore, and stop his agora gadflying (I know *that's* not a word!), but he didn't. He stood tall. He stood firm. He stuck to his guns and maintained that his only crime was ferreting out falsity and pretense where truth pretended to be. In modern-day parlance, his trial defense was something on the order of, "Hey, what do you want from me? All I did was take a bunch of arrogant somebodies and demonstrate that they were investing in falsehoods instead of truth. I showed up, asked some questions, and then asked some more questions. It's not my fault the answers were unsatisfying. I angered the wrong guys and now they're trying to screw me over. But I'll never stop exposing them. Never, I tells ya!" Good defense, right? Solid. Unyielding. Courageous!

The jury found him guilty by a vote of 281 to 220. So close!

Now it was time for the sentencing portion of this dramatic farce. The death penalty was on the table, but Socrates had a chance to suggest his own punishment. Surely this is where he asked for mercy, right? Not exactly. He said the jury should reward him for his services about town, and he asked for a high honor: membership at a local club for bigwigs. Nope. Didn't fly. When someone asked if he wanted exile, he blew that off as well. He was a man with a mission, so no, he wouldn't be silent or move away. The way he figured it, people would seek him out for conversation anyway, and he'd be right back where he started. In the end, the jury voted 361-140 for the death penalty and—WAIT! Where did those other 80 votes come from? How could folks who just a few minutes before voted him innocent suddenly want him dead? I'll leave that for you to decide. Let me know what you think!

Anyway, Socrates was in no mood to leave town or beg for his life. He loved Athens, and even though Athenian courts imposed an unjust sentence upon him, he was willing to literally take the medicine. He refused an escape plan and drank his cup of hemlock instead. His death was his ultimate victory. Don't believe me? Well, do you know the name of all his accusers off the top of your head? Go ahead. List them out. I'll wait. Do you know the identities of the folks who wanted him to leave town? Anyone? Do you remember all those who hated the great Athenian gadfly? No. But you know Socrates—the man who littered the marketplace with the shredded arguments of great pretenders.

Yes, Socrates Was a Brilliant Pest. Does It Matter?

That's Socrates in a very tight nutshell. Why did I take you on this side-trip to ancient Athens? Well, I know we said before that we are our own measures of proof on the spiritual and self-improvement paths, and we should strive to get past definition when it comes to religion and all those other assorted categories. Right now, you're probably thinking that Socrates is contradicting all of that with his questioning, proofing, and gadflying. But I disagree.

The point of Socrates and his incessant questions isn't to shame you, dissuade you from your path, or get you to keep quiet. Quite the contrary. Socrates provides a useful reminder to question values and foundations, even in a work in progress. You don't have to justify your personal search to anyone in the agora. Just make sure you understand why you're doing what you're doing. It's okay to explore and have fun, but make room for a little discipline. Check in with yourself occasionally. Challenge yourself. Put your own knowledge in the pan and pepper it with questions to see if you can understand it better or, perhaps, discard it in favor of something else. Why are you skipping temple this weekend? Why are you signing up for a lecture on angels? Why are you taking on the practice of meditation? Don't judge. Just ask. Go and do. But also, examine. See where these things fit in your life, and why. If something doesn't serve you, why are you still doing it? If something does serve you, why aren't you doing it more? Don't be afraid of questions. Don't be afraid of gaps in your knowledge. If you find one, examine it. Fill it in. If your beliefs are coherent and authentic, it will be reflected in a still mind and peaceful spirit.

I also mention Socrates because I want you to know that there are questions about the good life that can come from other than the religious or the spiritual. Did it matter whether Socrates believed in the gods of Olympus? Did it matter if he was a monotheist who believed in only one god? Do we have to care about that? Socrates stood for a few things that are (or should be) universal. He said: a life unexamined is not a life worth living. He said that the only thing he knew was that he knew nothing. He probably believed that a good deed and good virtues are their own reward. Socrates may have had a personal spirituality or religious belief, but in so many ways he transcended religion and spirituality and moved dialogues of great importance into the sphere of the practical and ethical. Maybe this has the ring of Confucius. Maybe this has a hint of the Buddhist. Maybe this feels like the Ten Commandments in some way. Getting the picture? Your proud atheist neighbor keeps his hedge trimmed. Your Muslim coworker got you a card for your birthday. Your Hindu client sent in that fruit basket. These aren't only the deeds of the religious. They are the actions of people living a life of *good*, across boundaries and beliefs. These are the doings of people who stand for something, and who know what they stand for.

Okay, Socrates Matters. Damn That Gadfly!

Do we live according to Socrates's tenets—at least the ones I've listed? I would argue that yes, we do. I would suggest that even without our awareness, we are students of the great philosopher himself—a true champion of regular folks (religious or not) searching for meaning, truth, and the good. Hopefully at this point in the book you believe me. But just in case you don't, let's go through the great exercise again. Oh, and by the way, these are only distilled points from what is a much more complex system of philosophy. And even if a philosophy professor wouldn't forgive me for my brevity, Socrates probably would, and that's all I care about anyway.

1. *A Nobody knows that the only thing he or she knows is that he or she knows nothing*: Do me a favor and return to my college calculus class with me again. Sitting in that classroom, fighting with numbers and ego, I thought I knew what I wanted out of life. I wanted to be a doctor, and I needed to pass calculus. When I walked into class on the first day, I knew that I knew virtually nothing about math, save for how to make change for a buck. But I knew I could pass. I barreled ahead with full steam while the Ds and Fs piled up. Eventually, I was asked to leave. At that point, I knew that was the end of my life, until I found that classics course I told you about, and I just knew I would be an archaeologist. That was, until I got sucked into law school. Fine. I knew I would love being a lawyer. I *knew* it. I *just knew* it. Until. Until, until, until.

The point is, we only think we know what we want or what we can do until something else comes along to prompt a question or test our knowledge. We go through life believing we have all the answers until we are proven wrong. Then we give in to the mystery. It's there where we start to receive true knowledge. Once I surrendered to life and the flow—because I realized I couldn't predict anything with certainty and really knew nothing about the grand plan—things opened up for me in ways I couldn't possibly imagine.

Think of it like this: the only thing you can possibly know is that you don't really know what's going to happen. Children won't always do what you expect, and friends will occasionally let you down. Any day could be the day your deepest beliefs are challenged, and any moment could be the moment your heart stops beating. A random book, song, or sculpture can enlighten you, and a chance encounter can destroy or create a cherished belief. These things happen to us all the time, usually when we're most comfortable in what we think we know. If you don't pretend to know all the answers, you are open for answers to come to you in ways you might not expect. If you don't always have to be right, you are more comfortable with being told you are wrong and engaging in productive dialogue to find truth.

Look, Socrates may not be 100 percent correct—there may be some things we know, like how to walk a straight line or boil water for soup. But don't get into the habit of believing your own hype on every subject under the sun. It's a mystery, man. Learn to live in it once in a while. The answers we collect on our paths to self-knowledge and growth are nothing compared to the power of constant questioning.

2. *A Nobody knows that the unexamined life is not a life worth living*: How's your job? Good? Good enough? Are you happy, or just comfortable? Are you stable in your life, or have you just learned to hold on to the handrail?

I have a friend who wants to get into management at her company so she can change things. Why? Because she did some soul searching and realized that her company is destroying the morale of employees to the detriment of clients. She wants to get ahead so she can pull others up with her. She has a great position and could just be comfortable there, but she realizes that there is a way to make a positive change—that she can get happy at work and bring others along for the ride, if only someone would take a minute to think about the process of better business. For her, *the unexamined business is not worth conducting*. She's going for it, thank goodness. Do you do that? When was the last time you examined family relationships that are currently on auto-pilot and tried to improve them? When was the last time you examined your room and threw out the useless garbage? When was the last time you surveyed your cluttered mind and tossed the extraneous?

Unexamined lives are filled with silent screams. No matter how many times we tell someone our life situation is good, "good" remains a wooly term that can substitute for "lazy" or "comfortable." I know you know how to investigate things. Do some examining and see where you are. Still good?

3. *A Nobody knows that a good act or being virtuous is a reward in itself:* I made a commitment a while back to overwhelm others with positivity. I don't always succeed in this endeavor, but I try. Sometimes people are so filled with rage and anger that kindness just sets them off even more. What then? Keep doing it. I try to smile at folks as often as I can. Very rarely do I get a scowl in return. When scowls do come my way, I try to remember that it isn't my mood that is making the other person frown, but their mood. And still, I try to smile and be positive. Why? If I practiced kindness and positivity only to get a kind and positive response, I'd be disappointed a lot of the time. Like you, I sometimes pick up slack or do tasks for others that are not on my list. I take care of a detail that goes unnoticed, but don't expect kudos. It makes me feel good. The deed's the thing. And when I fail? Well, then I forgive myself quickly because other rewards are just one more good deed away.

In the end, when all of Socrates's incessant questions are just a memory, what you'll have left is your own shining truth. Your own clear motivation to pursue your personal goals. Don't get caught up too much in proving things to others, creating artificial boundaries, getting defensive, or being right all the time. You might miss some great stuff while you're busy making demands. We're all in this together, and we need each other more than we need our differences.

Book of Socrates Meditation

Help me to examine my life with a critical and objective eye that is open to the new and renewed. Help me to do good for others while knowing I am doing that same good for myself. Help my mind to understand that I truly cannot know anything, for there is no solid ground of knowledge upon which to stand. Oh, and don't tell my kids about that last one. I want them to think I'm right about *something*, just because I told them so.

NOBODY'S EXERCISES

1. Do you have friends who don't share your religious or spiritual views? If you do, how do those relationships enhance your life?

2. Have you ever had a strange thing happen like what happened to my father and me? If so, did that experience have an impact on you?

3. What do you think of Socrates? Was he an arrogant and reckless pest or a man of integrity who was right to call out others on their ignorance?

4. How do you examine your life on a regular basis? What makes your life worth living?

5. Fill in the prompts below with your thoughts on some of these great thoughts:

A Nobody knows that the only thing s/he knows is that s/he knows nothing:

A Nobody knows that the unexamined life is not a life worth living:

A Nobody knows that a good act or being virtuous is a reward in itself:

Your own meditation:

The Book of You

Another Nobody Bible
(or Something Else Entirely) in the Making

The time has come. You've heard a little about my journey. You've studied the journeys of some ancient folks who inspired generations. There are gods and goddesses, ways and means, and rituals and prayers. You've read a bit, thought a bit, and (hopefully) laughed a bit. Now it's time to put it all together in your own book.

Nervous? Don't be. You've already done so much. If I haven't convinced you by now that you already know most of the things presented in this book, then I just don't know what to do.

What's in a Name? A Lot, Actually!

Let's start slowly. The first thing you can do is choose a title. I called mine *The Nobody Bible*. What name do you want? *The Dude's Tao? Barbara's Book?* I'd suggest making up something of your own, because my two suggestions stink. But hey, it's not up to me, right? This is for you. You won't offend anyone. And if you do? Well, tell them to make their own friggin' book. Try to capture the essence of *you* and the essence of your personal connection in the title. Make it three words. Make it thirty. This is a book of what, how, and who, with a sprinkle of "why?" thrown in to boot. Don't be afraid to get crazy. When you have a title in mind, write it below.

The name of my great life masterpiece is:

It's Only a Movie

There. You got it! Oh, wait, someone out there didn't write anything. That's fine. Take your time, person who didn't write anything. Don't sweat it. That blank isn't going anywhere if I did a good job with book layout. But if you are one of the folks who did get something down on paper, I'll bet that title has been in you since the very moment you bought this book...or picked it up from the floor where your friend was using it as a doorstop. I had you write it here so that you would remember it when we get to the real meat of this chapter. If you didn't get anything down, make a mental note and come back to it.

Alrighty. The title is there. Or not. Whatever. Now we are going to get down to the nitty gritty. We're going to create that personal masterpiece you can share (or not!) with friends and family and pass down through the generations. Or, if you want, you can just scribble through it like a fifth-grade homework assignment. That doesn't matter. The point is, we are now going to get all nice and disciplined and compile the knowledge you've gained throughout this book, as well as much of the knowledge you've gained in life, and construct your very own...whatever you've called it.

You can do this all in one sitting or break it down into weekly assignments. If you are working in a group or in pairs (much encouraged), then take some time to discuss each section. If you are working alone, meditate on each part and really touch the core. It's not too late to change your answers from previous chapters. That's why we're doing this again, see? Come to think of it, it's never too late—not even when you've moved on to another book. But even if the answers are the same, write them again. I can hear the collective groan, but trust me—the more you write your truth, the more you own it. As you write, you may discover small changes or nuances that you didn't see, feel, or notice before. This exercise should be how *you* want it to be, and it should be fluid and fun. Don't make it a chore!

I remember once when I was a young, horrible child of six-ish, I helped Dad prune some bushes on our front lawn. It was hot and boring work, until I decided to take up a pair of shears and poked Dad to see how many times I'd have to do it to get an "ouch!" Turns out, not that many! Oh, we had a great time after that, running around and around the house screaming. See? Even the most boring job can have the ring of fun under the right circumstances. Remember that advice. That's important.

I'm repeating this before we dive in: you've already done the hard work following each chapter. You can leave things blank if you want. You can add in your own stuff. You can completely ignore what I've written, cross it out, and fill something in on your own. See? Not so bad. Just follow the prompts to refer back to the substantive chapters above (or the stuff you wrote on those downloaded pages from thenobodybible.com) and take it away!

The Book of You and Your Life Masterpiece!

I. I'm _____ and this is my

personal masterpiece of me.

II. In the beginning, there was me. I don't remember much of my past before I was alive, and I can't say that I predict the future with 100 percent accuracy. I live my life according to principles gleaned from years of being alive. The most important influences in my life have been:

III. I live. I breathe. I am. I believe in the good life. To me, the good life is (Book of Beginnings, Question 2):

PEACE & plenty
freedom to go anywhere, do anything
give others what they need

IV. As for "religion" and "spirituality"? I define these words as I see fit. I may follow a religious or spiritual pathway. I may not. For me, these two words are defined as follows (Book of Beginnings, Question 4 & Book of Spirit, Question 1):

religion = rules/dogma
Spirituality = personal relationship
w/ the Sacred

If I am a person for whom God, god, gods, spirituality, or religion does not guide my life, I choose a different path. If you ask me what that path is, I might tell you this:

Awakening to Truth

V. I've gotten this far in life in spite of myself, yet, very much on purpose. I have my own contemporary views on great teachings of the past. Examples? (Book of Socrates, Question 5):

My view on: the only thing I know is that I know nothing:

Absolutely agree - except - Love Is All There Is

My view on: the unexamined life is not a life worth living:

agree: otherwise we are Robots

My view on: a good deed or virtue as a reward in itself:

it warms my heart

VI. I know things change. I know nothing really ever stays the same. But I've learned to adjust to the changes in my life. Here are some examples (Book of Buddha, Question 1):

As for "suffering," I know about it because I'm human. I also know how I define it and how I handle it. This is how I've learned to define and engage suffering (Book of Buddha, Question 2):

SKIP fr now

The Noble Eightfold Path is a guide for living. I may or may not be Buddhist, and I may not be perfect, but I have set my feet upon this path in my own way. Here's how I do it (Book of Buddha, Question 3):

My right understanding:

My right intention:

My right speech:

My right action:

My right work:

My right effort:

My right mindfulness:

My right concentration:

Armed with the understanding that I do follow some, or all, of these eight steps, I know I can bring positive change to the world and end a little of the world's suffering. I do this by (Book of Buddha, Question 5):

VII. There are a few special things in this life for which I would make great sacrifice. They are (Book of Jesus, Question 1):

The people I love

There is simplicity in this life—simplicity that shows us the clearest roads to our goals. I know that being decent doesn't mean being complicated. I have a few simple principles that guide my life. These are principles that motivate me to do the good I do in the world. Some of these guiding principles are (Book of Jesus, Question 2):

Jesus taught us to love the idea of god (whatever that is for me) and to love one's neighbor. These were the Two Great Commandments. I have my own conception of the "divine" or the "ultimate," and I have my own conception of what it means to be a good neighbor. I show my love for the *ultimate* by (Book of Jesus, Question 5):

doing what Love would do as often as I can.

I show love for my *neighbors* by (Book of Jesus, Question 5):

If I had to pick Two Great Commandments to guide my life, they would be (Book of Jesus, Question 4):

1. *some word*

2.

VIII. I understand the concept of yin and yang in my own way. In other words, I know the feeling of balance, and I know what balances me. Even if balance is not the state of all my days and all my thoughts, I have had balance in my life. When my life gets out of balance, here are some ways I act to restore it (Book of Confucius, Question 1):

get quiet
examine thoughts
remember what matters

I have had some great mentors and relationships in my life, and there are figures to whom I look for guidance—people who have taught me something about life or love. I will list some of them, including what they have taught me (Book of Confucius, Question 3):

There have been many such people
but not all good 'or happy
lessons

I know what it means to be a gentleman or gentlewoman. Here is my understanding of the term and how I try to embody it (Book of Confucius, Question 5):

Unfailing courtesy good manners treat everyone w/ respect

Confucius taught that a harmonious society was based on the Five Great Relationships. I understand that those concepts aren't just for ancient China. They work for me as well, even if they are not an exact fit. Here is how I see them at work in my life (Book of Confucius, Question 6A):

My ruler/subject:

My parent/child:

My older sibling/younger sibling:

My husband/wife (or any loving relationship):

My friend/friend:

I also understand the role of Confucian virtue. I may not play the flute or write calligraphy, but I have my own ways of expressing these values. They are (Book of Confucius, Question 6B):

My ren:

My shu:

My li:

My xiao:

My wen:

IX. I see the complementary dichotomy between yin and yang—between passive and active, cool and warm. I know that I embody two sides within me. I know I am a person of balance, and I respect both ways. The following are some ways I honor my need for quiet and simplicity in my life (Book of Lao Tzu, Question 2):

We all arrived at this moment by virtue of those who have gone before. I may or may not have descendants, and I may or may not have people who want to remember me. Nevertheless, I have wisdom. What follows is some of the wisdom I have learned that I would want to leave for future generations (Book of Lao Tzu, Question 4):

Peace is attainable but you must commit. Commit to it. There is no room for pettiness and ego crap.

Three main concepts and symbols in Taoism include the Tao, wu-wei, and water. One is the way of life, one means to take actionless action, and the other represents going with the flow of life. I have my own concrete thoughts on how these elusive concepts operate in my life. What follows is my own understanding (Book of Lao Tzu, Question 5):

Skip for now

My Tao:

My wu-wei:

My water:

X. Moses guided his people through the desert to a promised land. In fact, it was a guiding promise that kept the people strong. It was Moses's leadership that held the people together. I also have leadership qualities that assist me. I've led. Really. Below is a short list of examples (Book of Moses, Question 5):

I know that there are things in my life I need to wash away so that I can grow stronger and reduce my anxiety. Without necessarily naming names, what follows are examples of situations or people that I need to wash out while I float away in my ark (wait, isn't that Noah?) (Book of Moses, Question 2):

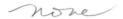

The Ten Commandments are ethical precepts meant to guide us. Whether or not I believe the hand of some god is behind them, when I read them, I see their relevance to the modern world (or not). Here is my take on these ten chiseled rules (Book of Moses, Question 6):

My Commandment 1 -- Have no other gods before me:

My Commandment 2 -- You shall not make an idol:

My Commandment 3 -- Don't misuse God's name:

My Commandment 4 -- Remember the sabbath day and keep it holy:

My Commandment 5 -- Honor your mother and father:

My Commandment 6 -- You shall not kill:

My Commandment 7 -- You shall not commit adultery:

My Commandment 8 -- You shall not steal:

My Commandment 9 -- You shall not bear false witness:

My Commandment 10 -- You shall not covet your neighbor's property:

XI. Suffering (this again?!) is a concept that shows up in more than one religion. It is a wheel upon which we spin until we find release. I want release from suffering. What follows is an example of something in my life that brings suffering, as well as one small, positive step to help me stop the wheel (Book of Brahman, Question 2):

none

Karma is also a common theme in the play of life—from reaping what we sow, to having actions revisit us in another life. I haven't always been a perfect person. Below is an example of a time when I may have fallen short (dang!), as well as an example of a time when I made amends (yay!) (Book of Brahman, Question 3):

too many to pick just one

Hinduism is full of interesting concepts, including the idea that our individual soul (Atman) is actually part of something much bigger (Brahman). There are consequences for our actions (karma) that determine our suffering (samsara) or release (moksha). Furthermore, there are pathways (yogas) that can yoke our carts to the path of escape from suffering. I have my own understanding of these complex ideas. Here they are (Book of Brahman, Question 5):

skip

My Atman and Brahman:

My samsara and moksha:

My karma:

My bhakti yoga:

My karma (yoga):

My jnana yoga:

My raja yoga:

XII. We live in a world of possibilities, where I am the measure of my personal experience. Intuitions, messages, and coincidences are everywhere, whether or not we believe they come from any divine source. I have my own examples of times when I was struck by something quite out of the ordinary. Here are my thoughts on that (Book of Muhammad, Question 1):

I understand the concept of "submission" in my own way. Maybe it's about surrender. At one time or another, we have all been forced to give in and accept something or someone. What follows are examples of times when I simply had to lay down my ego and go with a situation. Also included is an example of a place in my life where I need to do that now (Book of Muhammad, Question 2):

Self-sacrifice can mean sacrificing the ego to ask for help. It also means providing help at personal cost or giving up things we love for the benefit of another. It means maintaining an internal and external cleanliness that shines in the light of the sun. What follows are my understandings of some key concepts of sacrifice (Book of Muhammad, Question 5):

My prayer:

My charity:

My fasting:

My purity:

XIII. There need not be God or gods to have inner harmony. Both formal or informal rituals can help me discover the personal core of peace and balance. I know I can create my own way of being in the world—a way that brings me comfort. What follows are examples of activities (or inactivity) I can add to my daily regimen to help me maintain personal balance and stability (Book of Spirit, Question 3):

We all have obligations to fellow travelers and to ourselves. Below are ways that I help to heal the world, heal myself, and try to connect with what is true and real for me each day (Book of Spirit, Question 4):

My world and self-healing:

My connection to the inner self in the everyday:

XIV. I know not everyone will agree with me all the time. I know that my views on religion, spirituality, and personal growth as I define them (or exclude them) won't always be in line with every person. In the end, I know what I feel and I know what I've experienced. I examine my life and know what makes me tick. What follows are some ideas on my life motivations, and why I think mine is a life worth living (Book of Socrates, Question 4):

When I am confronted about my beliefs in a negative way, called "silly," or meet someone who chooses screaming and arguing instead of rich dialogue, I will remain calm and open. Here's how I can handle that situation, in order to maintain my sanity in a world of conflict:

XV. I may have teachers, mentors, books, poems, art, music, or other inspiring things in my life. These are where I turn when I need to find that sweet breath of inspiration. Below are examples of what brings me joy or strength when I need it:

XVI. Finally, I know that throughout my life there will be ups and downs, challenges and joys. What follows is a phrase of my own creation that I can use to guide me when the light grows dim or the road seems long. Or it is an affirmation of gratitude that can carry me even further when the winds of blessing are already blowing at my back. It is drawn from my knowledge of the world, my knowledge of myself, and the knowledge that I have my own mastery of some of the world's most important and influential concepts. It is mine to share or hold as I see fit:

The Book of Endings

Can't We Just Say New Beginnings?

Here we are. We have reached the end of this journey together. I admit, I didn't think I'd be this emotional. Look at all you've accomplished! I'm proud of you. I knew you could do it (not that you cared about that or anything...I just felt compelled to tell you).

I hope you see now that "nobody" is nothing more than a marker. A metaphor. It sprang from an unexpected string of personal conversations, reflections, and thought exercises that arose in my life and congealed in my mind as a personal movement of self-improvement. I am so happy you've allowed me to share it with you. The "nobody" concept has encouraged me to try to transform my ordinary life into something positive and special—using the simple tools and pieces of wisdom that are already around me. I looked to the past to find out what religion and philosophy had to say about self-improvement and growth, and I examined spirituality to see what contributions it could make to a life in progress. I was quite pleased to discover that I was already living so much that is so rich and powerful. And by the way, so were my friends, family, students, clients, and total strangers. We all have something meaningful to contribute, even though people may not know who we are. We don't need special permission to believe what we believe, and we don't need to buy into anyone else's stuff to make a positive change. We just need to be people in the world, doing what we do.

"Nobody" is zero. A place to start. An empty vessel waiting to be filled. A blank canvas awaiting the brush. It's positively pregnant with possibilities! Remember: my neighbor doesn't know me when I first move in. To him, I'm nobody in particular until I shake hands and introduce myself. Over time, through conversations over the fence and cups of sugar borrowed, I become a person with unique attributes and characteristics that separate me from just another person in the neighborhood behind a closed door. Come to think of it, we are nobody to ourselves until we do a little self meet-and-greet. We must experience and engage our own lives and beliefs before we can truly start to understand who we are. Simple, right?

You already know how to live the good life. You can be kind, you have innate and powerful ethics, and you have much to contribute. We in the crowd make the church donations, cook the latkes for the Hanukkah party, and give the alms to the begging monk. As you search for your own truth, call yourself what you will. Be what you will. Go where you will. Just make it fulfilling. Be an active participant in your own life, a decent member of greater society, and a positive steward of humanity. The time is now, and we are all nobody together. *We are the movement. We are* *the believers. We are the wise. We all matter.*

The Journey Continues

We Might as Well Travel Together

Thank you so much for reading *The Nobody Bible*. I hope it brought you some insight and entertainment! If you'd like to continue the adventure, please visit thenobodybible.com.

If you enjoyed the experience, please consider posting a review on your favorite book or social media site. It's important that we all share our thoughts, and I'd like to hear yours. You can reach me at info@thenobodybible.com.

Notes

The Book Before the Books

1. *Weltschmerz* is a really fun German word. Look it up! Oh, and look up *Schadenfreude* while you're at it. No particular reason. Just for kicks!

2. Sometimes I'll capitalize God and sometimes I won't. Sometimes I'll say "god," and sometimes I'll say "gods." More on this in later chapters!

3. We said this in fine print on the copyright page, I'm sure, but it bears repeating. Nothing in this book is intended as counseling or professional advice. If you need help with any kind of physical or mental health issue, please consult a specialist. Sometimes that visit can be the path that leads to roads you never imagined.

The Book of Beginnings

1. The Pew Research Center website has a lot of great information on religion and public life. It's a terrific resource. I used it to get some of the statistical information in this chapter. See: *http://pewforum.org/Other-Beliefs-and-Practices/Many-Americans-Mix-Multiple-Faiths.aspx*.

2. Pew again! http://www.pewforum.org/2015/11/03/u-s-public-becoming-less-religious.

3. Pew it to me one more time! *http://www.pewfo-rum.org/2016/10/26/one-in-five-u-s-adults-were-raised-in-inter-faith-homes/.*

4. See Note 1, above.

5. Don't worry if you're confused by all of this. Lots of folks are. Defining religion is really difficult. In my classes, I ask students to share their definitions on the first day. It's amazing the variety we get! Search the internet for "defining religion" and see what sorts of interesting things you discover. Feel free to share your definitions with us over at thenobodybible.com!

The Book of Buddha

1. Dates for historical figures can vary widely. I'm just going with what I'm going with. If you find something different, great! Oh, and please note that for dates I'm using B.C.E. (before the common era) and C.E. (common era). I didn't want to use B.C. (before Christ) or A.D. (*Anno Domini*—in the year of the Lord). There's all kinds of commentary on this in books and on the internet. Check it out!

2. I use the term "Hindu" as one of convenience. "Hindu" actually refers to a family of beliefs in Indian religious tradition. For more, see my note below under *The Book of Brahman.*

3. The Oracle of Delphi was a priestess, Pythia, who served the Greek god Apollo. You could come to her and ask her your burning questions. She would take your gold, sniff in some kind of gas from the earth, and tell you things about the future. The problem? Her answers could usually be taken two (or

more!) ways. I was in Delphi once. I spent a night in a youth hostel during the first snow of the season. I slept under five wool blankets and still froze my oracles off.

4. This goes without saying (and, in fact, I say it back in the chapter): I'm not giving you health advice here. If you have a health issue, see a trusted specialist and hear what they have to say. I did what I did in consultation with specialists, not by ignoring them.

5. As you can imagine, there are many schools of Buddhism. I'm just taking you on the general tour. Research a little about Buddhism and see what you can discover about gods, spirits, salvation, and rituals. You may be surprised at the variety.

6. Despite the near-death experience, Mesa Verde was a really great place to visit. Look it up!

The Book of Moses

1. All Biblical quotes in this section come from *The King James Bible* in the public domain—not from the Bible I found in the hotel drawer.

2. I'm going to capitalize "God" (and attendant Biblical references to "Lord") in this chapter when it relates to the discussion of the Jewish God, because that is the convention in the Bible as it relates to the sacred narrative. However, I'm still not going to capitalize every godly pronoun. So there!

3. Muslims believe that Ishmael was the true firstborn to Abraham and that he was the forefather of great Arab tribes. They

believe Muhammad, the prophet of Islam, was a descendent of Ishmael. Indeed, in Genesis 21, God promises Abraham that he will make a great nation of Ishmael.

4. Yes, I know I'm using male pronouns for God. Personally, I'm more of a "he or she" kind of person, but I'm doing this for readability.

5. I'm not capitalizing "sabbath" throughout this book. The Bible I'm using doesn't capitalize it, so I'm trying to stay consistent. But that doesn't get you out of anything!

The Book of Confucius

1. There is debate out there as to whether Confucianism and Taoism are religious pathways or philosophical traditions (remember when we talked about the difficulties in defining religion?). I'm not going to delve into that distinction here. These traditions have a long history in religious studies departments and comparative religion textbooks, and I'm going to consider them here as religious traditions with strong philosophical cores. Whether they fall neatly into one camp or the other in no way detracts from their rich treasure troves of wisdom.

2. I know you know this, but it bears repeating: the heart of much religion is deep philosophy, and that spirit helps drive this book! See Note 1 just above.

The Book of Lao Tzu

1. You can go ahead and pronounce "Tao" like "dow." Oh, and if you meet someone who spells it "Dao," you can be friends. That's an acceptable spelling as well.

2. All excerpts from the Tao Te Ching in this chapter are from *The Tao Teh King, or The Tao and Its Characteristics,* by Lao-Tse (as translated by James Legge in *Sacred Books of the East, Vol. 39,* (Ed. by M. Müller), 1891), in the public domain.

3. Buddhism is also a member of this Chinese religious family. It perhaps forms a triplet instead of twins. Confucianism, Tao-ism, and Buddhism have exerted great influence in China (and beyond!) over the years.

4. There are many ways to spell this name. You might see Laozi, Lao-Tzu, or Lao Tse. There are probably more, and I think that's pretty great.

5. I pronounce this "woo-way," but I'm guessing there's a more proper way. Ask your friend who speaks Chinese, and then let me know.

6. I'm sure wind had a hand in this as well, but I'm no geologist. If you're curious about it, I encourage you to head to the Grand Canyon and see what the fuss is about. I guarantee that no matter how grand you imagine it, it is so much grander.

The Book of Jesus

1. I'm going to refer to the Holy Land as "Israel," even though people called it different things through the ages. Look around the internet and see what folks have to say about this issue. Very interesting. Search "What was Israel called during the time of Jesus?" or something like that.

2. The term "messianic" or "messiah" comes from the Hebrew word for "anointed," as in anointing royalty with oil or consecrating something holy with oil. Jesus's followers often refer to him as "Christ" (the Greek term for "anointed") or "messiah."

3. All Biblical quotes in this section come from *The King James Bible* in the public domain.

The Book of Brahman

1. I'm using the terms "Hindu" and "Hinduism" as a convenience for readers—and for myself! For a more robust discussion of these terms, please take a look at the myriad sources available on the internet. There's some interesting stuff out there!

2. From *The Upanishads*, by Swami Paramananda (Translation and Commentary) (1919), in the public domain.

3. From *The Upanishads* (as translated by Max Müller in *The Sacred Books of the East, Vol. 1*, 1879), in the public domain.

4. See source in note 3 above.

5. References to the Bhagavad Gita in this section from *The Song Celestial; or Bhagavad Gita,* translated by Sir Edwin Arnold (1885), in the public domain.

The Book of Muhammad

1. All references to the Koran in this section from *The Koran,* translated by J.M. Rodwell (1915), in the public domain.

2. You can check out the link to the *American Time Use Survey Summary* here: http://www.bls.gov/news.release/atus.nr0.htm.

3. All Biblical quotes in this section come from *The King James Bible* in the public domain.

A Further Note on Sources

Religious-text quotes in this book come from sources in the public domain. As you can imagine, translations vary greatly. I encourage you to do your own investigations and to further research the passages you enjoyed. Surf around to find other versions of what I've presented here, or head to your local library or bookstore. The journey of a billion pages starts with a few verses with which you really connect!

Acknowledgments

This book would not have been possible without years and years of study, discussion, tears, and laughter with some truly authentic and gifted people. Thank you to my wonderful family, who never doubted that something could come from a series of endless nothings. To my editor (you know who you are!), thank you for reading countless drafts and being a fountain of enthusiasm and fantastic ideas no matter how many times I gnashed my teeth and resisted. To my teachers, clients, and students—you jumpstarted my mind and spirit, and I'm eternally grateful. To the Michaels, who knew I would write this book and this line, thank you. Finally, to my partner in this life—I...um...well, you know.

Made in the USA
San Bernardino, CA
19 June 2018